MESSING
UP THE
PAINTWORK

1 3 5 7 9 10 8 6 4 2

Ebury Press, an imprint of Ebury Publishing
20 Vauxhall Bridge Road
London SW1V 2SA

Ebury Press is part of the Penguin Random House group of companies whose addresses
can be found at global.penguinrandomhouse.com

 Penguin
Random House
UK

Copyright © Ebury Press 2018
Research and captions by Tom Clayton
Design by Estuary English

First published by Ebury Press in 2018

www.penguin.co.uk

A CIP catalogue record for this book is available from the British Library

ISBN 9781785039850
Printed and bound in Great Britain by Clays Ltd, Elcograf S.p.A.

MESSING UP THE PAINTWORK

THE WIT AND WISDOM OF

MARK *E.* SMITH

A CELEBRATION

EBURY
PRESS

Editor's Note

WHETHER MARK E. SMITH'S death in January 2018 prompted feelings of loss, or fond memories, or simply piqued your interest in the life and work of the great man, I hope this book will contain something for you. In looking through the vast archive of available material on Mark, I've tried to paint a portrait of the man in his own words and in the words of those who met and admired him. We've also included new essays, poems, sketches and tributes, intended to highlight the artistic legacy that he leaves behind.

Mark may be gone … but The Fall will live forever. TC

'I can't look back like some fans can. I can't get beyond the fact that most of it was shit …'

Renegade

MES

Stuart Maconie

So I take my Dixons portable tape recorder from my bag and place it on the table but before I can even phrase my first question Mark E. Smith seizes upon this –

"Where d'you get that? I want one of those. I went into a little Asian electrical shop in Prestwich to buy a tape recorder like that; something to get my ideas down and the bloke said "You need this, sir, a little mini cassette recorder dictation device" and I said no, mate, I want one that takes ordinary C60 cassettes. I could be in Oslo, I could be in Naples or Chicago and I don't want to be faffing about trying to get hold of those little tiny cassettes …

'And he says "Oh sir, you are living in the past. These are what everyone uses now. And everywhere sells the tapes, everywhere …" So I said, go on then, give us one of those recorders … and you'd better give us ten of those little tapes.'

And he says "Sorry, sir, we don't sell them"!'

MARK EDWARD SMITH became one of the most storied figures in British popular music without ever becoming a celebrity. He was not a star in any accepted sense of the word. It was entirely possible to live a life as a pop music enthusiast and never have seen him perform live or on screen, or perhaps even to have heard his work at all. The Fall never appeared on *Top of the Pops* and their biggest selling single, a cover of someone else's much bigger hit, only reached number 30 in the UK charts. But MES will always remain legendary in a way that many of his better-known and more richly remunerated rock peers might even conceivably envy a little, even as they park the Maserati in a Knights-bridge mews far, far from Prestwich.

Stories abound, and those stories are mostly terrific. Like most people who knew him even a little, I have scores of vignettes like the above. But just as journalists are encouraged never 'to let the truth get in the way of a good story', we shouldn't let the stories, good as they are, get in the way of the truth. Mark E. Smith was irascible, aloof, funny, belligerent, wayward, slippery, complicated and smart. But he was more than just a character. He was also a very real creative talent responsible for a unique strand of modern British art: the music of The Fall.

The punk upheaval was, as a hundred thousand generic articles have pointed out, necessarily purgative, primitive and bracing, a litter-strewn cyclone of rancid urban air, a rough beast slouching towards the estab-lishment bent on sedition. The Occam's razor of punk thinking may have been crucial and necessary in a music scene sedated and de-politicized and largely in the hands of a tedious, neutered transatlantic aristocracy, but much of punk's actual music qua music was and is terrible. It's hard to imagine anyone other than lime-haired nostalgists listening to Eater, Chelsea or 999 for pleasure now. The Fall's music was engraved upon this boilerplate of loud, insistent, inexpert primal sound but soon acquired a dimension of its own, spectral echoes of krautrock, glam, northern soul, even country. But what set it furthest apart were Smith's words and his persona.

In their baffled and faintly sniffy obituary of Mark, *The New Yorker* said that his main contribution was 'to liberate the rock lyric from the need to make sense'. This was bunkum. If you grew up in Manchester in the benighted 70s and 80s, songs like 'Kicker Conspiracy', 'The NWRA', 'Totally Wired' and more made perfect sense. Stewart Lee opined in a valedictory piece that The Fall in their late muscular hard rock phase reminded us of music's power 'to bypass sense'. Paolo Hewitt, a met-ropolitan soul boy tasked with reviewing them for *NME*, once bemoaned their 'brutal and nonsensical music'. From friend and foe alike, there's been an eagerness to stress the absurdity and surrealism of Smith's writing. But that's not what I hear most. I hear Wyndham Lewis and Kafka, a bitter, diamond-hard Modernism, or Vonnegut and Phillip K. Dick, the amphetamine clarity of a hyperactive, restless mind.

The crucial division in British society today, the cleave that affects how you vote, how you view the world and your place in it, what you think about Brexit and politics is not race, class or gender; it's whether you went to university or not. John Lydon didn't. Morrissey didn't. Nor did Curtis, Weller, Rowlands, nor MES, though he was surely smart enough. In fact, none of that rebarbative, objectionable, voluble generation of autodidacts that built the post-punk musical world did. This is perhaps the most significant fact in their shared histories. None of them inculcated the mild liberal consensus that has become ubiquitous on the artistic left. On a visit to the *NME* once, hearing and seeing a record by The Verve and gazing at vocalists Richard Ashcroft's lank hair and vacant expression, MES remarked famously 'God help us if there's a war'. The derogatory term snowflake as now used to describe sensitive young liberals is felt by many to be unfair, dismissive and offensive. Perhaps. But it is certainly a term I can hear MES using, three pints and a few Jamesons into a long afternoon on licensed premises.

One of his last TV interviews was conducted on such premises with Channel 4's Krishnan Guru-Murthy. During it, Smith wondered why so many of Manchester's Syrian asylum seekers were young men. 'Why aren't they staying and fighting? Good job my dad and granddad didn't do that with the Nazis'. A kind of goldfish-mouthed apoplexy ensued from many disappointed admirers unable to comprehend the fact that MES came from a different world to theirs and was made of entirely different stuff. He was not just there to shake up the suits at Radio One. He was there to confuse and confound the middle class indie children of Peel as well, to challenge all their smooth unthinking orthodoxies.

His attitude to work was similarly proletarian, mistrustful of the boss class (despite being one himself within his band) whilst candid and sardonic about his own background, community and neighbours. He was part mischievous shirker, part Arthur Seaton hedonist drone, part self-made entrepreneurial small business man. He hired and fired and ran The Fall like a back street garage or Mike Baldwin's garment factory. He was unpredictable, individual and happy to cause offence. In fact, he was utterly committed to the very Modernist notion that giving offence to the comfortable was part of the duty of the artist, the need to *épater la bourgeoisie*. He did this partly with scorn for the establishment – he said the music industry had become 'a middle class executive business like the police force' – and partly through a kind of hippie-baiting streetwise ultraconformity. The three star jumpers beloved of working class northern soul fans and footie lads. The kind of smart leather jacket that wouldn't get you refused entry at the Labour Club. The crisp white shirts. The deliberate use of archaisms like 'courting'. The injunctions to 'pay your rates … and pay your water rates'.

A unique mind and voice who was also the purest product of his class and region at very particular time in its social and cultural history, it's hard to imagine we will see his like again.

God help us if there's a war.

MES and I are in the bar of the Ramada Hotel Manchester. We are waiting to be joined by Peter Hooton of The Farm and Paul Heaton of The Beautiful South to discuss and review the singles of the year for the *NME*'s Xmas issue. In the few minutes before they arrive, Mark disposes of four pints of strong lager. (At the end of the day, the bar bill will nudge £1000 and The Farm will have to cancel a show that night because of Hooton's 'indisposition'.) The first record we listen to is 'You Can't Touch This' by MC Hammer, who is essentially a novelty rap act, a six foot plus black American man in baggy harem pants. Mark E. Smith looks at his portrait and then at me, and then sips his pint thoughfully.

'You know, Stuart. You've got a bit of a look of MC Hammer yourself.'

When The Fall emerged from Prestwich, Manchester, no-one had heard anything quite like them before. *Live at the Witch Trials*, their scabrous debut album released in 1979, was met with widespread acclaim, and marked the arrival of a new hip priest in town – one with plenty to say. Mark's uneasy relationship with the press continued throughout his career; he could be charming or explosive, but the results were invariably fascinating.

New York City, 1985. *Laura Levine/Getty Images*

Search: Mark E. Smith

Remarkably there are a lot of them,
even though the middle E
was meant to mark him out from all the other Smiths.
According to socials he's either
Recruitment Manager at a well-known online retailer
(you'll know the one),
a North of England University Vice-Chancellor,
Actor slash Violinist slash Singer,
Water Resources Lecturer –
tweets are his own –
Mobility Superstar,
author, speaker,
everything mobility his passion,
sounds organiser
from Denver, Colorado,
election boycott advocate – don't vote! –
learns Chinese Kung Fu under Siu Barry Gray,
Newark, New Jersey,
Christian music lover,
reluctant teacher,
married to Queen Laura,
the most wonderful woman ever,
one year older than he was last year,
or the real Mark, uncommon,
gone, and what will we all do now?

Paul McGrane

MARK E. SMITH (22) vocals. Founder and lyric writer. Called a dictator by many. Audiences love him ha ha. Has problems at dry cleaners viz; 'How did your coat get like that, Mr Smith?' 'What do you do for a living!'

Rowche Rumble press release, July 1979

'Mark Smith never sings anything you'd expect. And what he sings doesn't mean what you think it does.'

Steve Hanley,
The Big Midweek

Meeting your heroes
Phil Harrison

I SPENT MUCH of my childhood confused. When I was nine, my family moved from Wakefield in Yorkshire to a picture-book village in the Cotswolds. Identities are nowhere near fixed at that age but even so, I always felt like a displaced Northerner. When you spend a fair proportion of your early adolescence being teased by posh kids for having an ecky-thump accent and supporting Leeds United, it prompts a certain chippy defiance. Salvation arrived in the form of The Fall, and their frontman, Mark E. Smith.

The Fall's channelling and occultising of the North was ingrained and unmistakable. But crucially, it also refused to be definitive. What I loved about Smith wasn't that he was a clichéd, flat-capped, flat-vowelled Northerner but actually, that he was none of those things. He was many other things instead, none of which I'd imagined were compatible with each other. He was a beer-drinking, Rothmans-smoking aesthete. He was the embodiment of a particular cultural identity even as he refused to be imprisoned by it. He'd read books and he'd worked on the docks. He was simultaneously instantly recognisable and deeply exotic – his lyrics and the music he somehow coaxed and cajoled out of his revolving pool of musicians rendered northern England, the place I somehow felt I belonged, bleakly mystical and sullenly magical.

In my early 20s, I did something that Smith would never have counte-nanced and moved to London. Skint and under-employed, my early days in the city were spent trudging the streets of Camden Town and King's Cross, scowling at 'lickspittle Southerners' with The Fall's 'Smile' play-ing on my Walkman.

By the time I was in my mid-30s, this laughably stagey alienation had abated. But my love of The Fall certainly hadn't. By now, I was a freelance journalist; when the opportunity to interview Smith for *Time Out* arose, I was excited and terrified in equal measure. I can honestly say that I have hardly ever, before or since, felt as nervous as I did in the 15 minutes before that interview. Imagine if Mark E. Smith thought I was a prick and decided to tell me so? You don't come back from humiliations like that, do you? Never meet your heroes, particularly when they drink heavily and have been known to stub cigarettes out in journalists' faces.

Smith was everything and nothing like I'd expected. He was already on the lager at around midday. He helped himself to my cigarettes, swore spectacularly, resisted flattery. He carried a tangible air of unpredictability; not menace exactly, but a sort of blunt, unsparing rigour. There was an un-mistakable edge, certainly – Smith was the most unbiddable of men, never feeling the need to sell The Fall or himself to anyone. It's hard to imagine that his company was ever relaxing – he was too intense for that and occasionally, he'd refuse to fill an uncomfortable conversational space; leave you hanging.

But even so, there was a strong sense of submerged warmth – he asked if I was 'courting' and wanted to know which other bands I'd interviewed recently. He was also hilarious – dry, sarcastic and brutally unsentimental. He possessed a maniacal, cackling laugh that exploded without warning, his whole body surging forward from his chair.

I honestly can't remember much of what we talked about and I've long since lost my copy of the interview. But I don't really care – plenty of Mark E. Smith interviews exist, almost all of them better than mine. Really, the commission was a means to an end: I just wanted to shake his hand and have a beer or two. I'm absolutely certain I was just another London media twat to him but even so, he was kind enough not to show it. He was, in fact, of all the strange things he could have been, thoroughly likeable. Confounding to the last, then – even after the interview, the enigma lived on. I imagine it always will.

'Smith's invective seems to come from somewhere outside the class system: a vantage point from which everything seems equally absurd … Smith's withering gaze scanned the whole of society, and found only grotesquerie.'

Simon Reynolds,
Rip It Up and Start Again

'What surprises me in life is how little people have to say.'

Melody Maker, March 1990

'Someone sent me a copy
of Damon Albarn's 'Heroes
and Villains' he did for your
paper, so, like, if you want
my real list just reverse
his choices. Heh heh heh!
Except for the National
Front, don't you dare put
that down, you buggers.'

NME, December 1993

Summer 2004: MES at the Malmaison

Tim Cumming

IN JANUARY 2004, I'd published a feature with the *Guardian*, 'Wild Thing', interviewing former members of The Fall – long before David Simpson's *The Fallen* was conceived. This was partly on account of Mark being on holiday with his new wife, Elena, when I had put in my bid for interview time on the release of the excellent *Country on the Click*. Given the frequency of Fall albums, it wasn't long before I got a chance to talk to him later that Spring, after a US tour, and in the midst of a seriously needed reissue programme.

The Fall had been the first and best part of a double bill with the overly proficient Magic Band at the Royal Festival Hall, and I had reviewed that for the Independent ('MES saunters on to the voluminous stage of the Royal Festival Hall, drops his jacket by the drums and sets about dismantling his mic-stand, and over the next hour he sets about recreating the off-hand menace of a Fall gig by cuffing his bass-player, twiddling with the amps, poking mics into the drumkit and delivering a three-note keyboard solo with his hand behind his back, his body corkscrewed, like some malevolent modern-dress Richard III').

Shortly afterwards I placed a feature with the *Independent* (to be published as 'Fighting Talk' in May 2004). Sometime in April I made arrangements, boarded a filthy and decrepit Virgin train – in league against me – to Manchester Piccadilly. I'd been told to go to the Malmaison bar. I did. It was about fifty paces from the station entrance. And there I was, thinking I might end up in Salford. I later learnt the place was owned by Mick Hucknall. The comedian Bill Bailey was in the bar, looking like his publicity photo. No MES. Stripped down, steel-finished, and an insect din of voices. I took a table near the window, view of the door, the street, pints of lager. MES came down the slope from the main door on crutches. I hailed him, got drinks, and we drank, smoked and talked for a long afternoon. I gave him a copy of one of my poetry books. It was called *Apocalypso*. He like the title, took it with him as he left with a snapper who was shooting some pix on a nearby railway bridge, then came back saying, 'this is really good.' I gave him a few other books over the years – *The Rumour*, *The Rapture*, *Contact Print*, each one from a different small indie publisher, a bit like the more erratic periods of The Fall's discography.

Although I had in my head all these foggy second hand tales of MES stubbing out fags in journalists' eyes, that wasn't the man or the artist I met. He was friendly and funny, a fascinating gentleman, soft spoken, much given to laughter, uninterested in addressing prosaic questions, always on the ball when it came to more freeform talk about art and music and the body politic. I think that with MES, what you got from him was what you brought to the table. It helped to know your stuff, and not to trust the internet. We drank and talked until his then-wife, Elena, came to join us. Soon, they went off in a cab, I skulked around the station a bit. The days of transcribing from those lo-fi little tapes was a nightmare, but meeting Mark was a dream, really.

The next time I met him, in a weirdly straight bar at the top of Piccadilly, he said, 'I didn't realise it would be you.' The last time we met, we finished off in a big dark, empty late afternoon pub, of the older, heavier kind, drinking tequila. He had a weird smile hanging off his face, his back to the window, in silhouette. It was like looking at someone laughing in outer space. There was no sound. I remember him at one point reassuring me that 'I'd not end up in prison'. Thanks for that, Mark.

Coda in conversation, 2013

'I don't get any phone calls any more on the landline. You can tell when the mobile phone bill's come in, you don't get any calls for two weeks. I feel sorry for them. Because it does damage your brain. The ministry of defence said that. Wi-fi, it's the equivalent of putting a little cockroach in your brain, that goes right through your brain and comes out the other side after laying an egg. It rots your brain. Who are they talking to and what are they talking about? I don't understand it.

Nobody likes us, Tim, that's why.'

'The Saddam Hussein of rock, the bastard's bastard.'

Steven Wells, *NME*, August 1990

'I've read a lot of *NME* interviews and I can see all the groups just pandering to some kind of left-wing philosophy. I don't like it ... I don't care if *NME* readers don't vote me bleedin' top of the poll. I don't give a shit.'

NME, November 1984

'I walk around the street like this
(spreads arms into Messianic pose)
with "I'M FROM THE FALL" on me
forehead, but they ignore me.'

NME, September 1992

'I think you guys are encouraging
Mark to be like this. You journalists
love it.'

Shane MacGowan, February 1989

'I can't grasp that "Ah" thing. It's just having a go at me for my accent. That's easy, that's lazy. I could do that to you ... I don't laugh when I see it in the *NME*, no. I think it's quite sad.'

NME, 1995

'People have forgotten how to drink. Proper pubs went a long time ago. It used to be, if you were stressed, if you'd had a row with your wife, you'd go to the pub for an hour, sit down and sort it out in your mind. You can't do that now ... TVs everywhere, fucking tortilla chips.'

Select, September 1996

'Mark E. Smith is best understood as a 1970s disco-misfit descendant of Victorian fright-writers such as M.R. James or Arthur Machen. He runs his group like a displaced medieval Lord of the Manor, by turns loopy and cunning, and writes in an eerie, distorted, splenetic argot all his own, which perfectly encapsulates his contempt for, and his fascination with, a world he did not make.'

James Park, *Cultural Icons: Cult Figures Who Made The Twentieth Century What It Is*

'I just swear at the TV basically.'

Answer to the question 'What does Mark E. Smith do to relax?'
Toronto fanzine, circa 1994

'Mind your own business. Hold on. CAROLINE, HAVE YOU GOT A CIGARETTE? I'VE GOT TO DEAL WITH THIS FUCKING BASTARD ASKING ME QUESTIONS! Ahahahaha! Did you hear that?'

The List (Scotland), June 2000

'If I was to go round and apologise for everything I've ever done I wouldn't have any days left in me.'

Renegade

'He's not the easiest man to shop for, partly because you know that whatever you get, it'll be wrong. The things I've bought him over the years ... The year of the tankard we all pooled our money and I went out on a limb, coming up with the idea of a personalised drinking vessel ... It was of high-quality silver, exquisitely hand-crafted in Cambridge by one of the world's most revered silversmiths ... "Comes in very handy ... late at night I have a piss in it and throw it out of the back door into the garden. At the squirrels to stop the fuckers eating my fence."'

Steve Hanley, *The Big Midweek*

Manchester, 17th October 1987. *Steve Pyke/Getty Images*

'The trouble with the monarchy is that they're revoltingly middle-class ... They haven't got the style, even the Queen. Charles is in fuckin' London and he goes, "Look at the way people are living, summat must be done about the inner cities." And the cunt owns fuckin' Cornwall! He could do summat about it tomorrow.'

Select, May 1993

'The *Daily Mail* is full of shit ... it's funny, sometimes you pick it up and you think it's the same one you bought a month before. You could probably trade it in for the same one and nobody would notice.'

Melody Maker, March 1990

'Having a problem is like a professional career these days. It's become really hip. People actually don't like it if you haven't got a problem. The country's turning into a bunch of whingeing, mithering bastards – going on about nothing at all.'

Vox, March 1994

'I always vote for the stupidest name on the ballot. No, I haven't voted Raving Loony – you don't fucking get Raving Loony candidates in Salford. You get things like Orthodox Jews For More Pavements In The Area. They always get my vote.'

Q, May 2001

'After hesitantly whispering an incomprehensible story about some long-ago, shady, spy-like confrontations within the abandoned Czech Embassy across the street – then unsuccessfully attempting to erase it from my tape recorder by rewinding it and tapping on it with a fork – he gets to the concepts behind the new album.'

Mark Blackwell, *Spin*, October 1993

'BT changed the phones around in my house and it's a real bastard: I've got to phone from the hall now, but I've noticed it's made me friendlier. I don't know if that's a good or bad thing.'

Q, April 2000

'We've got a website, but when people try to explain how it works I go blank … [and] e-mail: it takes so long to send one it's like etching a gravestone. It takes an hour! You can write a letter in a tenth of the time.'

Teletext, November 1997

'I never use them portaphones. My wife has one and all me mates have 'em. They're always trying to make me get one, but what do I want a portaphone for … no portaphones for me. No thanks.'

Word, January 2006

'We were on tour in Europe when Saffron handed out her carefully typed wedding-present lists of Habitat houseware, complete with codes to ensure guests' personal lapses of taste wouldn't interfere with her décor. At the bottom of the last sheet was Mark's only request: he'd scrawled "some blank cassettes".'

Steve Hanley, *The Big Midweek*

'It's easy to slip into nostalgia ... the '70s were crap. The '60s were crap. The '50s were crap, even though I was only two.'

NME, February 1998

'I might get knocked down tomorrow, it's not my problem. If you want to be wise and rich when you're 60, who fucking cares? Good for you.'

Guardian, April 1999

FOR ALL THE REASONS we might feel compelled to, it is impossible to set Mark E. Smith apart from his art. Smith is his art: hypnotic, uncompromising but without pretence, doomed. Smith is a scene at the end of the night; 5am, when the party has died and the sky is beginning to pale and all that's left is a handful of hopefuls gathered around a kitchen table, scattered with crushed cans and shrouded in cigarette smoke, listening to someone monologue about late capitalism. There is thrill and a sense of salvation, yes – but there is also violence. For Smith, that violence shot outward through his music and at those closest to to him, but also turned inward. His palpable sense of destruction – like his music, a patterned chaos – is what prompts us to dub him both a reluctant genius and a terrible bastard. But if there's anything we can take from Smith's work it is to reject our tendencies towards binaries and idolatry. His lyricism is both obtuse and revealing – faithfully documenting working class Northern life while lashing out at the oppressive social constructs around it; feverishly wringing every last drop out of life while calling it all a load of shit. Over their 41 years The Fall have seen enough members pass through their doors to form a small congregation. Pain and admiration run through the band's history in tandem and form a foundation of nuance, of detail, that can't be ignored or cherry-picked from. Unparalleled in every way including their flaws, The Fall are an incredibly human band. You have to take it all, or it's nothing.

Emma Garland

THE RISE OF
THE FALL

Mark's unique slant on music and songwriting would endure for far longer than many of his contemporaries, and often saw him abruptly parting ways with record companies who tried to meddle with the band's output. The Fall's cryptic lyrics and liner notes, hypnotic riffs and unconventional production methods often left critics beguiled or bemused – in thrall, like the rest of us, to a singular and indomitable musical vision.

'I think I've got an advantage over musicians in that I know nothing about music and suspect I'm tone deaf.'

Vsign, late 1979 / early 1980

Mark flies home to Baby
For Mark E. Smith

You were on my cassette up in my ears with your
violence. My walkman was a scratchy portal straight
to your gammy mouth. I liked it, and the tight sound
of the drums, mounted with the skin of pigeons.

I was also frightened but not of anything.
The time the kids spat on my woollen shelf and
stoic as a pink sparkler, I knew you knew. In your
tank top, casting flames from your ancient hanky.

Something dumb and vicious that ran through all of it.
The ditches laced with porn-distaste in the kitchen,
I knew it. In our world apart, the southern quarters,
we knew the flailing, social hurt. I hid in woodlands

and heard the silence, we were better after all. You
in the gnarled old roots, a latchkey in the darkening
cover and I, proper with my bronze spoon, my
residuals, my uncanny face all flattened by

witches and tarmac. Now gone, into the farflung
corners of the disco-cosmic gargoyle. Rings
of smoke around your ankles like A-OK, and
up in your thorax, the flickering burden of joy.

Emma Hammond

'With our stuff, I don't want to make it faultless like, 'cos then you've just blown it ... There's bits where I'm trying to catch the band out, where I'm fighting against the band for them to do something off the wall 'cos it's more interesting to me.'

Printed Noises, 1980

Performing at The Ranch, Manchester's first punk club, 18 August 1977. *Kevin Cummins/Getty Images*

'Most of it sounds like Smith put paper bags over the microphones. His voice blares out of the group's ramshackle, elephantine locomotion in a way that insists on your concentration. After all, any word could be vital.'

Richard Cook, *NME* review of *The Wonderful & Frightening World of The Fall*, October 1984

'This is a very funny track. It's a pity you can't hear what's going on.'

Mark on 'Impression of J.Temperance', *Grotesque* press release, November 1980

'What I want is a well-produced bedroom sound, to get the things that are confidential, but that you lose when you have to shout, to keep that noise value and still retain that excitement.'

One Two Testing, June 1986

'When you write you should do your best, you know, not just like some kind of deep, self-centered monologue that is boring to everybody. I always try and put a little crack in it, and I always try and put lyrics that mean nothing and like jumble it all up.'

Mark in *Tape Delay* by Charles Neal

'[W]e were going to call ourselves The Flyman And The Fall. I was going to dress up as a greenfly and stand in front of the band going buzzzzzzzz … When we'd do interviews, if someone asked me a question I'd reply, Buzz.'

Sounds, July 1986

'My penchant has always been for words. I care about them and I want them to look good on paper before I sing them. A love song written down just doesn't look good to me.'

Jamming!, November 1984

'A lot of these bands in the North of England just try to copy what we do, so they have these stupid titles for their songs, like "Man Locked In Fridge Saga" or something ...'

Only Music, November 1986

'I also think it's a boring, bourgeois thing to put lyric sheets in records. I find that most people who print lyrics are arrogant and stupid. It's hilarious to read these lyrics that they think are good.'

You Can't Hide Your Love Forever, Winter 1989

'They were born, like all great rock'n'roll, out of clumsiness and chaos. Repetition was their rap, but it never became their trap.'

John Wilde reviewing *Extricate*, *Melody Maker*, February 1990

'His force of personality is matched only by the force of nature that is Fallmusic. Still going after almost thirty years, they've accumulated a body of work whose sheer size and density rivals Dylan's. A body of work like a body of water – never ending and ever shifting, its "changing same" ceaselessly turns up scintillating new patterns. You never step in the same river twice, they say, and so it goes with The Fall.'

Simon Reynolds, *Rip It Up and Start Again*

'He looks like The Black Adder and sings like a dog in pain.'

Ron Rom, *Sounds*, October 1985

'If you're going to play it out of tune, then play it out of tune properly.'

Renegade

'The Fall is the bane of my life as well as the best thing in it.'

Select, 1990

'I kind of expected it but hoped otherwise.'

'Guitarist Ben Pritchard said there were chaotic scenes at the maverick frontman's send-off.'

The *Daily Mirror* reporting the brawl at Mark E. Smith's wake.

Flickin' the Vs
in a v neck jumper your mother bought.
Bruises stamp the passport,
an accent that's a border.
Pan Book of Horror Stories,
an escape from the one you live in every day.
Comedy that's all set up,
every laugh a put down.
Every step is a drag
and speed rots your teeth.
There's a hand on your shoulder,
a jump in the heart.
The heraldry of pub bouncer tattoos,
ever the set to you always lose.

Tim Wells

'By the late eighties, little could be done to salvage the English-based music system: a bleak future lay ahead subsistent mainly on recycled Dylanisms, courtesy of gentlemen whose main point was: "Because of my handsomeness, you never took me seriously as an intellectual – for that you and audience suffer!"'

NME Christmas message, December 1985

'It's amazing the effect the press has. I've seen bands crying over reviews, like their whole life was destroyed. Some of my favourite reviews are bad ones!'

NME, January 1980

MIND ROCKER

THE FALL
Bend Sinister *(Beggars Banquet)*

AS FAR as recording techniques go, The Fall seem to aspire to playing live in front of a solitary microphone in a padded room in a crumbling building in a boom town. Where The Fall hang out you're in touch with the past (when 'Bournemouth Runners' gets into gear you'll swear the Totale turns) but with the future under your thumb. The world crumbles, parties, battles and dies. And it's all just fuel to Mark Smith's fire.

How close they get to recording with just one microphone (and it would have to be a big, square BBC mike) isn't clear, but most of the ten tracks were recorded almost directly onto tape (at Abbey Rd). So Bend Sinister has a massive thrust and a degree of spontaneity which makes The Fall sound like some American '60s 'garage' band who've only just got together and shaken it. There's shuddering surf-guitar and sawdust-strewn vocal pitched in with some of the most incongruous sounds; including computer-game bleeps and Wurlitzer organs.

Fading are Smith's Babel-ling monologues of eyeball-to-eyeball social comment, now replaced by more occasional contributions; pithy, scratchy phrases delivered in so clotted a vocal style that they undermine any potential accessibility in the music.

Some tracks seem more like rough sketches, and others are the coolest mind-rockers you could ever want to shake your head to. Like most Fall LPs the songs vary in mood and musical tone, but there's always a recognisable Fall sound. And the best way to define 'the Fall sound' is to say it sounds a good deal better than the rest.

The Fall survive and prosper because they're never where anyone else is; they're a step to one side or a step ahead, or just hiding, working, waiting.

From the sombre casualness of 'British Grenadiers' to the strong beat-thrash of 'Mr Pharmacist', 'Bend Sinister' drags us into a world there's no escaping from. But on this you don't feel the hard edges, the bite and the snarl you would have felt from their early releases.

'Shoulder Pads' is a crazy piece of wobbly-necked Yuppie-crushing 'bubblegum' (Simon says), which finds Smith in brilliantly self-mocking mood. 'Terry Waite says' is a short, but far from sweet investigation into the motivations of *'Mr Big'*, the Archbishop's Special Envoy (and Brix gives a squeal).

'Realm Of Dusk' sounds like Link Wray with a lot of big problems, and 'Bournemouth Runners' – which starts with whispered words and *'trouble on the horizon'* spurts into a song about a lad who used to follow The Fall from pillar to post in an attempt to steal their backdrop; and finally (apparently) he gets away with it in Bournemouth. Of all places.

'US 80's and 90's' is built on a beatbox, and goes on to guide us through all the things we're losing out on as Western society clamps down on beer, cigarettes and whisky. People telling other people what to do has never gone down well with Smith. No one can stand comparison with The Fall. In the half-light of the late 20th century, they beat the retreat, show us our way backwards through the realm of dusk. And through the dog-eared pages of Roget's Thesaurus Mark Smith chases the English language; with an axe.

Dave Haslam

NME, October 1986

Machete Head

Daniel Cockrill
Illustration by Daniel Weighill

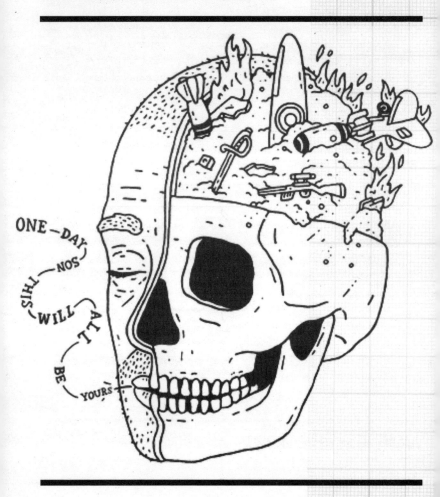

ONE-DAY SON THIS WILL ALL BE YOURS

A head full of swagger
A head full of sewer
A head full of clutter
A head full of scrap metal
A head full of hash
A head full of mustard gas
A head full of chips and peas
A head full of chimpanzees
A head full of killer bees
A head full of memories
A head full of distant planes
cutting through the sky
like death
A head full of blood
A head full of concrete
A head full of dead meat
A head full of Twitter feeds
A head full of nose bleeds
A head full of hateful
of heart full of spiteful
A head full of skin full
A head full of plutonium
A head full of buckets and bullets
of land mines and atom bombs
A head full of ethnic cleansing
A head full of mass graves
A head full of scowl
A head full scars
A head full of crushed cars
A head full of late bars
A head full of dead stars

A head full of static
A head full of rhetoric
A head full of sick
A head full of prick
A head full of smut
A head full of slut
A head full of scum
A head full of cum
A head full of cunt
A head full of can't
A head full of Kant
A head full of fuck
A head full of fascism,
racism, sexism, sarcasm
A head full of chasms
A head full of bad jokes
A head full of rape jokes,
racist jokes, sexist jokes,
homophobic jokes
A head full of fake laughter
A head full of empty laughter
A head full of echoing halls
A head full of stabbings
and sawdust
A head full of fever
A head full of medication
A head full of bent spoons
A head full of broken moons
A head full of war fear
A head full of warfare
It's lonely in here

53

'When people talk about The Fall's lyrics, they like to talk about themselves. They want to relate to something that isn't there. Like it's an open slate and they can write anything they want.'

Magnet, August 2004

'They can never be an influence because no one can progress on what they have done except The Fall themselves.'

Richard Cook, *NME*,
March 1982

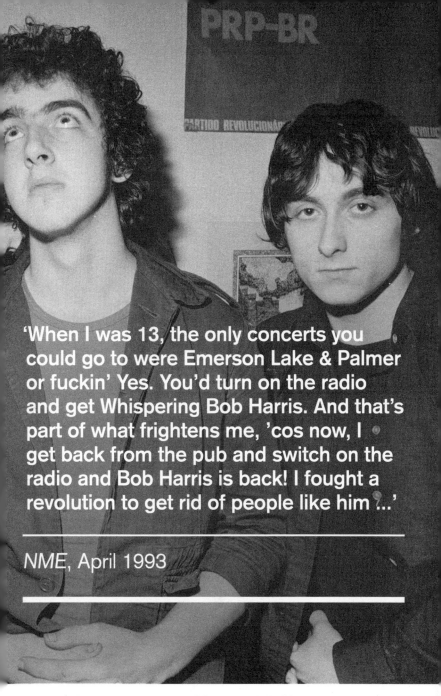

'When I was 13, the only concerts you could go to were Emerson Lake & Palmer or fuckin' Yes. You'd turn on the radio and get Whispering Bob Harris. And that's part of what frightens me, 'cos now, I get back from the pub and switch on the radio and Bob Harris is back! I fought a revolution to get rid of people like him ...'

NME, April 1993

Perverted By Language

Hayley Scott

THE FALL'S SIXTH STUDIO ALBUM, *Perverted By Language*, documents an epoch where the group had reached a pinnacle. There are myriad reasons for this: for one, it defines the sound of The Fall we know and love – the polyrhythmic presence of two drummers, the abrasive, oft-tuneless, twang-y guitars and the extraordinary detail of Steve Hanley's bass playing. At the heart of this record, though, is 'Garden' – a song that's as visionary as it is emblematic of Mark E. Smith's stunning turn of phrase. Here, Smith uses lyrics as an instrument, carrying the song in a way no other vocalist could.

To some, 'Garden' is long-winded, stagnant and too much at odds with the comparative optimism of the likes of 'I Feel Voxish'. To me, each component of the song feels vital, necessary. On the surface it's dark, disorientating and cynical, but there are glimmers of something softer – poppier, even – at its core. Driven by a melody that's sentimental, with lyrics that are contemplative (contrary to Mark E. Smith's infamous disposition) the song has facets that are rare in the music of The Fall, but work sublimely.

Much like on previous albums, Mark E. Smith's lyrics are cryptic and absurd to the average ear. But the way he takes apart the English language and creates his own interpretation of a narrative is nothing if not astonishing. Here, lyrics veer from poetic and introspective (See: 'Garden', 'Hotel Bloedel') to some of the simplest, most accessible songs he's written (See: 'Smile', 'Eat Y'Self Fitter'). While Smith's cutting discourse underpins every song, it's reductive to solely credit him for the strength of this album. That would undermine the blunt brilliance of the musicians: Paul Hanley and Karl Burns are an unfailing union – their collaborative drumming unveils a more tribal element that attempted to recreate the visceral savagery of live performances. Moreover, without Craig Scanlon and Steve Hanley's contributions, *Perverted By Language* would be remembered very differently now. For instance, the two members are the driving force behind one of The Fall's most prescient songs: the peculiar brutality of 'Eat Y'Self Fitter' is a result of the interplay between the tough rigidity of Hanley's bass lines and Scanlon's sharp and salient guitar riffs. The two fall like meteorites around Mark E. Smith's assimilation of modern alienation.

This album is also the point of intersection between two very different groups, with songs debuted live in the Riley era and Brix Smith's new energy and material appearing in the mix. Brix's pop sensibility, anchoring the music, would encourage Smith to defy lyrical conventions with ever-greater linguistic experiments. See 'Garden' for conviction: Smith uses words to – almost – tell a story, as opposed to relying on aesthetic devices or catchphrases. Fall commentators have a tendency to negate the dark humour in Smith's lyrics, too, but there are few lines as skilfully witty as: 'He had a kingdom of evil book under a German history book, he was contrived like that.'

Despite Brix's influence, most of the album was recorded without her, but nevertheless she makes her mark on the leisurely 'Hotel Bloedel'. The first track to ever feature anyone other than Mark E. Smith on lead, the song offers an unfamiliar, strange beauty in which two worlds collide: Brix's tuneful refrain and Smith's poetic surrealism are conflicting but neither one would work without the other.

Elsewhere, the languid, casual stroll of 'Hexen Definitive' utilises Smith's affinity for Country and Western, and. Smith's dalliances with various musical styles are realised throughout the record: the motorik essence of Can can be heard on 'The Man Whose Head Expanded', 'Wings' and 'I Feel Voxish' while the stop/start arrangements of 'Eat Y'Self Fitter' – despite its idiosyncrasies – elicits something stereotypical of The Fall as we remember them now: with a predilection for chugging rockabilly. There are even very subtle tinges of The Velvet Underground at play on 'Pilsner Trail', despite the song's overt Englishness.

The present-day reverence for *Perverted By Language* is at odds with its general critical reception when it was released in 1983. In retrospect, one wonders if these critics were listening to the same record as you: '"Eat Y'Self Fitter" is standard DULL modern Fall. Rumble rumble groan. I think Mark needs new musicians,' writes David McCulloch of *Sounds* magazine. 'It's The Fall plodding on, going nowhere, MAKING DO,' writes another.

What seemed like an idle, downward spiral to critics then is now viewed as The Fall at their uncompromising best: Smith taking his irrational, instinctive love of a word, using and abusing it for implication, corrupting meaning, is what makes him the best lyricist, writer and poet of a generation. While other front men were relying on clichés and retrofitting old formulas, Smith was creating his own.

The singularity of Smith and The Fall meant they were more of an anomaly in 1983 than ever. While punk was the initial spark for The Fall, they rejected whatever trend came next. For context, one of the biggest selling albums of 1983 was Spandau Ballet's True – it's a strange world where such disparate records exist side-by-side. Just as post-punk began to fragment and New Wave became the New Thing, *Perverted By Language*'s vitriolic strangeness was the antidote to a musical landscape that was becoming increasingly insipid and gimmicky. Of course – with the help of Brix Smith – The Fall subsequently ended up on the fringes of mainstream success, even if Smith didn't want anything to do with the mainstream.

Perverted By Language might not be The Fall's biggest success story, but it's become a firm fan-favourite, for all the reasons critics used to dismiss it the first time around. It marries accessible post-punk with something far darker and meaningful. It's these nuances – the juxtaposition between light and dark – that bring the record to life.

ON TOUR

The Fall had begun essentially as a loose, semi-improvised venture which coalesced around Mark's writing. However, they quickly evolved into a ruthlessly controlled, highly dynamic, many-headed, almost constantly touring beast. The addition of a second drummer for what many considered to be the band's finest record, *Hex Enduction Hour*, saw the lineup regularly described as the greatest live act in the world. In subsequent years, they would write and perform the avant-garde dance piece *I Am Curious, Orange* at Sadler's Wells, and recorded countless sessions for John Peel's BBC Radio 1 show. However, touring often proved brutal for the band, with many iterations disintegrating on the road ...

Manchester, 1978. Left to right: drummer Karl Burns, bassist Marc Riley, Mark E. Smith, keyboardist Yvonne Pawlett and guitarist Martin Bramah. *Kevin Cummins/Getty Images*

'We did [The Fall's first gig] for this avant-garde music association, I remember that. Played with a socialist brass band. And a guy who made symphonies out of bird noises – great, totally surreal … [we] weren't even headlining, it was the bird noises, then us, then the brass band.'

NME, February 1996

'Let me introduce to our new bass player. He's from Yorkshire! And I am a patronising creep who will go to any lengths to win an audience.'

'This is our last song ...' (huge cheer) 'My one regret is driving here tonight.'

Danny Baker quoting Mark in a live review for *ZigZag*, February 1978

'Being onstage shouldn't be a pleasure, it should be like your craft. I don't consider it performing at all, performers are like other people to me. It's the same with writing too. There should always be a fear involved of what you're doing, a fear that maybe you shouldn't be there at all.'

NME, August 1986

'A bit faster this time; I know it's winter but fuckin' hell.'

Beggars Banquet press release for 'Oh! Brother', with Mark addressing Karl Burns

And a tow, row, row, row, row.
In memory of the Captain ...

1. Who gave life to words like 'Kentledge!'

2. Who used scat-sounds against Slaughter and the Dogs, for they ran out of lyrics in 'Cranked up Really High'. The Captain never ran out ... 'Ba ba me-oo me-oo'.

3. Who blew his nose on stage. Oh to have kept the tissue, and sold morsels to sinners! The Nightingales supported, in Country and Western shirts. Sheffield, 29th October 1981.

4. 30th April 1982. Retford. The Fall played the legendary 'Backdrop'. By 2008, I've established this. The support group were from Iceland: Don't forget the Cod War! (I'd feared my old man might be conscripted.) In the audience, punks and miners scrapped. It was hard, but it was merry.

5. In 'Garden', what got me was the gather-and-surge. Like, There's always more, where that came from! You'll not be left alone ... 26 years on, it was the power-surge in 'Slippy Floor': that got me like Yeats, Nineteen Hundred and Nineteen, Part VI – where he raises demons.

6. 7th Oct 1985, or was it 1597?, I saw the Cap and Brix on Princes Street, just above Waverley Station. He wore zipped boots, and looked like Allan ('Sniffer') Clarke – Leeds Utd No.8. Mrs McRae confused 'My New House' with Shakin Stevens' chart topper. At night we drank whisky and cloves.

7. Aug '88. The Captain left Tollcross Supa-Store with a bag of mini-Marathons and a pack of Superkings. His overcoat was good and he bore a doctor's bag. I didn't say hello on this occasion either.

8. There are far lovelier songs than 'Edinburgh Man', the gist of which was only that whisky was served in ¼ gill measures in some pubs in Fountainbridge. So a large Scotch gave you 1/8 of a pint – in England only $1/12$. $1/8$ is a drink, $1/12$ a kind of dampness in the glass. I will not list far lovelier songs.

9. The gigs at The Forum weren't up to much. Nonetheless, I saw myself in them.

10. Nov '98 at The Astoria. He tidied up after the group. They were young, and left their things all over the shop. My pal Nick Groom took this image away.

11. September 2014. I came upon Brix at a Route/Rough Trade event: Last time I saw you, you were rotating on a burger! She 'laughed'.

12. Let us pause on the Captain's total humour: the word for such humour is hilaritas. So I learned from the letters of Dietrich Bonhoeffer, hanged at Flossenbürg, April 9th 1945.

13. I've mentioned years and intervals and dates. So a genuine cult comprehends your time. You can measure yourself, without left-overs. A genuine cult also takes your time: think of Dragnet. Of course there was life before The Fall, but it was unredeemed – like the time of the virtuous Greeks.

14. 'Kentledge' is a word for ballast, something Captains know to be vital.

And green grow the hedgerows along the walls …

Michael Nath

'A blistering "Fiery Jack" started up. Now sparks really began to fly. Halfway through the song, Smith spotted a suitor climbing out of the audience and making up to his wife. Brix was mildly amused, Smith was positively psychotic. Under a hail of punches and blows the young romantic was mercilessly booted off stage and when a hired heavy arrived to take control, he too received a healthy kick from Smith's jackboot. Two numbers down and Smith was totally, totally wired. Not bad going. "At last we have something in common with you," he spat at the audience. "For we too do nothing all day." The place erupted with indignation.'

Melody Maker, January 1987, review of The Manchester Festive Party, a day of free live music for the city's unemployed.

'Amidst all this ruckus, Mark E. Smith stays calm, calmer than he's ever been; shit, Mark E.'s in love, and look, he's even parting his hair.'

Chucky Eddy, *Village Voice*, December 1985

IN 1988 THE FALL provided a soundtrack for, and played alongside, Michael Clark's dance company as they performed *I Am Curious, Orange* at Sadler's Wells in London. The ballet had a uniquely Fall-like sensibility; giant hamburgers, cans of baked beans and cutlery costumes all featured, in a pop-art reimagining of the story of William of Orange. The soundtrack, with the slightly different title *I Am Kurious Oranj*, featured 'New Big Prinz', a reworking of the fan-favourite 'Hip Priest' from *Hex Enduction Hour*, and a version of William Blake's 'Jerusalem' with added contemporary lyrics. Sadly, little footage now exists of what is generally agreed to be one of the band's most intriguing projects ...

Michael Clark and Company perform the ballet *I Am Curious, Orange* with musical backing by The Fall at the King's Theatre, Edinburgh, 20 August 1988. In the background are (left to right) guitarist Craig Scanlon, keyboardist Marcia Schofield, guitarist Brix Smith (on hamburger), drummer Simon Wolstencroft, Mark E. Smith and bassist Steve Hanley. *Kevin Cummins/Getty Images*

'The beauty of The Fall is that it just keeps changing … He throws things at us. You just have to get up there and play it.'

Brix Smith Start, *Sounds*, February 1987

'We're used to lead singers not talking to us much during their gigs – but only Mark E. Smith wanders offstage during songs, strolls round behind the drumkit as it takes his fancy, squats on the floor, back to the audience, still singing, still curdling the air with that unmatchable voice like a washing machine with some vibrators and a squeaky toy going round inside it. He is, on many levels, the one and only.'

Andrew Collins, *NME*, April 1992

'Helen you'd better learn to spell repetition if you're going to review The Fall!'

Kevin Cummins to Helen Ward, *NME*, March 1990

'Mark E. Smith is old, and he is wise, and he is grumpy. He is also a genius. It's handy to have one around.'

Caitlin Moran, *Melody Maker*, April 1992

'Mark Smith's only comment was to compare the trendy utilitarian decor of The Waterfront to that of an open prison.'

Adam Green reporting Mark's thoughts on Norwich, *Melody Maker*, November 1990

'I've played enough universities with The Fall and I wouldn't wish that lifestyle upon anyone – you know, having to live in places like Colchester.'

NME Student Guide, October 1998

'Oxford Street was bought to a standstill last Thursday when thousands of pencil necks and weirdos spilled out of the HMV Shop, where they were watching top Mancunian glam terror pop army THE FALL, and into the busy central London shopping area. DETECTIVE INSPECTOR PAT McCAT told Public NME that he was shocked at,
a) the popularity of the band,
b) the amount of people who queued up to get their copies of *The Frenz Experiment* signed, and
c) how the band didn't perform "C.R.E.E.P."'

NME, March 1988

'I have to be, frankly, dragged screaming to the airport to go on tour in America.'

You Can't Hide Your Love Forever, Winter 1989

'When we tour America, we get people coming up to us saying, "If only you could be a bit more like Talking Heads." Well, we always had better backdrops than Talking Heads.'

Frieze, September 1992

Right: On a bridge in a snowy park, 16 January 1981. *Kevin Cummins/Getty Images*

'They've only just lifted the ban on us at Glastonbury. I said something about CND – in *Melody Maker*, actually – and we were banned from playing or even going, which I thought was the funny bit. I mean, if the bass player goes down there who's going to recognise him?'

'We did one festival in Denmark, and they put us in a fucking cage! They had Jethro Tull on and all that shit, and they had tents for dressing-rooms, but because we were punks, they put us in this cage and locked us in!'

Melody Maker, June 1992

'We've been banned from every hotel in London, including this one, only they've forgotten about it. They say, one of the lads sneezed on this pillow, that'll be £55. Hotels in England are like hospitals where everything would be alright if all the patients left.'

Lime Lizard, July 1991

'His first request – aimed directly at the undisputedly well-bred talks coordinator – was for a bucket. To her undying credit, she treated this as the harmless whim of an eccentric genius. A bucket was found. After she had handed it to him, he put it on the floor in front of us and pissed into it, noisily.'

Michael Bracewell on Mark's appearance at the ICA, *Guardian*, November 2003

'Smith sauntering about the stage with icily calculated indifference only adds to the sheer rigour of the sound. He addresses nobody, but his delivery is fanatical. Anger breaks over its surface, but a Fall gig is a vital confusion of sound and meaning, signifier and signified, a theatre of clamour and impersonality. Sometimes you can make out his words, at other times not; it doesn't matter, the challenge to both heart and mind is there.'

Barney Hoskyns, *NME*, November 1981

'At The Fall's Camden Dingwalls show, the band invaded the stage during opening band Pacinos' set, forcibly removing them and disconnecting their amps because their set was too long. Surprisingly, Mark E. Smith was not involved.'

NME, November 1999

'John Walters wrote me a letter that said "You are the worst tuneless rubbish I have ever heard ... please come and do a session."'

The Wonderful and Frightening World of Mark E. Smith, BBC4 documentary, 2005

John Peel (1939-2004), 8 February 1972. Len Trievnor/Daily Express/Hulton Archive/Getty Images

The Fall Peel Sessions

Session 1, 30 May 1978: 'Futures and Pasts' / 'Mother-Sister!' / 'Rebellious Jukebox' / 'Industrial Estate'

Session 2, 27 November 1978: 'Put Away' / 'Mess of My' / 'No Xmas for John Quays' / 'Like to Blow'

Session 3, 16 September 1980: 'Container Drivers' / 'Jawbone and the Air-Rifle' / 'New Puritan' / 'New Face in Hell'

Session 4, 24 March 1981: 'Middlemass' / 'Lie Dream of a Casino Soul' / 'Hip Priest' / 'C'n'C – Hassle Schmuck'

Session 5, 26 August 1981: 'Deer Park' / 'Look, Know' / 'Winter' / 'Who Makes the Nazis?'

Session 6, 21 March 1983: 'Smile' / 'Garden' / 'Hexen Definitive – Strife Knot' / 'Eat Y'Self Fitter'

Session 7, 12 December 1983: 'Pat Trip Dispenser' / '2 × 4' / 'Words of Expectation' / 'C.R.E.E.P.'

Session 8, 14 May 1985: 'Cruiser's Creek' / 'Couldn't Get Ahead' / 'Spoilt Victorian Child' / 'Gut of the Quantifier'

Session 9, 29 September 1985: 'L.A.' / 'The Man Whose Head Expanded' / 'What You Need' / 'Faust Banana'

Session 10, 29 June 1986: 'Hot Aftershave Bop' / 'R.O.D.' / 'Gross Chapel – GB Grenadiers' / 'US 80's-90's'

Session 11, 28 April 1987: 'Athlete Cured' / 'Australians in Europe' / 'Twister' / 'Guest Informant'

Session 12, 25 October 1988: 'Deadbeat Descendant' / 'Cab It Up' / 'Squid Lord' / 'Kurious Oranj'

Session 13, 17 December 1989: 'Chicago Now' / 'Black Monk Theme' / 'Hilary' / 'Whizz Bang'

Session 14, 5 March 1991: 'The War Against Intelligence' / 'Idiot Showland' / 'A Lot of Wind' / 'The Mixer'

Session 15, 19 January 1992: 'Free Range' / 'Kimble' / 'Immortality' / 'Return'

Session 16, 28 February 1993: 'Ladybird (Green Grass)' / 'Strychnine' / 'Service' / 'Paranoia Man in Cheap Shit Room'

Session 17, 2 December 1993: 'M5' / 'Behind the Counter' / 'Reckoning' / 'Hey! Student'

Session 18, 20 November 1994: 'Glam Racket – Star' / 'Jingle Bell Rock' / 'Hark the Herald Angels Sing' / 'Numb at the Lodge'

Session 19, 7 December 1995: 'He Pep!' / 'Oleano' / 'Chilinist' / 'The City Never Sleeps'

Session 20, 30 June 1996: 'D.I.Y. Meat' / 'Spinetrak' / 'Spencer' / 'Beatle Bones 'N' Smokin' Stones'

Session 21, 3 February 1998: 'Calendar' / 'Touch Sensitive' / 'Masquerade' / 'Jungle Rock'

Session 22, 18 October 1998: 'Bound Soul One' / 'Antidotes'/ 'Shake-Off' / 'This Perfect Day'

Session 23, 19 February 2003: 'Theme From Sparta F.C.' / 'Contraflow' / 'Groovin' With Mr. Bloe – Green-Eyed Loco Man' / 'Mere Pseud Mag. Ed.'

Session 24, 4 August 2004: 'Clasp Hands' / 'Blindness' / 'What About Us?' / 'Wrong Place, Right Time'/ 'I Can Hear the Grass Grow' / 'Job Search'

'I had this idea that Peel was a starting point to better things, like the morning show.'

Renegade

'In the flow and jetsam of modern society, only John Peel stands out as the modicum of "respectability-alternative". Without John, all children would be weeping – their kindred looking towards heavens for signals, none apparent.'

Radio Times, August 1999

'Listen to a session a day before meals. You won't necessarily like it all, but you'll never forget it.'

Ken Garner, *The Peel Sessions*

THE FALLEN

Mark thrived on tension, both on and off stage. He realised early on that regular lineup changes were needed to keep The Fall both interesting and interested – and wasn't afraid to dismiss long-standing members with the same indifference he offered temporary stand-ins. The regular personnel changes eventually became a (wearisome) joke, with critics tending to forget that the band's core – Smith, bassist Steve Hanley and guitarist Craig Scanlon – played together virtually uninterrupted for almost twenty years; longer than many bands' entire lifespans.

The Lyceum Theatre, London, 12 December 1982. *David Corio/Redferns/Getty Images*

MARK E. SMITH
KAY CARROLL
LUCY RIMMER
ED BLANEY
MARTIN BRAMAH
CRAIG SCANLON
BRIX SMITH
ADRIAN FLANAGAN
TOMMY CROOKS
NEVILLE WILDING
BEN PRITCHARD
TIM PRESLEY
PETER GREENAWAY
UNA BAINES
YVONNE PAWLETT
MARCIA SCHOFIELD
DAVE BUSH
JULIA NAGLE
ELENA POULOU
MICHAEL CLAPHAM
TONY FRIEL
MARK RILEY
STEVE HANLEY
SIMON ROGERS
KAREN LEATHAM
ADAM HELAL
JIM WATTS
SIMON ARCHER
STEVE TRAFFORD
ROBERT BARBATO
DAVE SPURR
STEVE ORMROD
KARL BURNS
MIKE LEIGH
PAUL HANLEY
SIMON WOLSTENCROFT
KAREN THEMEN
TOM HEAD
SPENCER BIRTWHISTLE
DAVE MILNER
ORPHEO McCORD
KEIRON MELLING
DARREN GARNATT
PAUL BONNEY

1977 1979 1981 1983 1985 1987 1989 1991

VOCALS   GUITAR   KEYBOARDS   BASS   DR

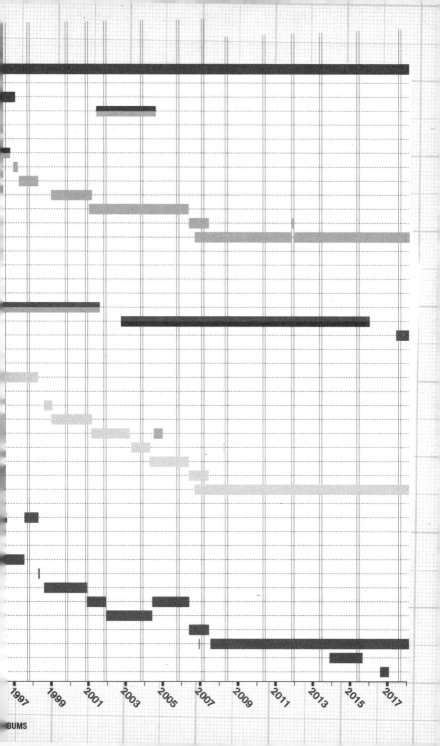

'My grandad used to stand outside prisons, wait for people to come out and say "come and work for me" … that's a bit like what I do with the group'

The Wonderful and Frightening World of Mark E. Smith, BBC4, 2005

'It's a standing joke in Manchester that The Fall are very deep and always arguing about things ... and it's true. There's never a common agreement within the band. Instead there's a tension that makes us stronger.'

Malcolm Heyhoe interview,
NME, March 1978

'He was a bit of a witch, a psychic, a warlock – he understood energy intuitively ... we were all the disciples in a way. We were like the hypnotised masses behind Mark.'

Brix Smith Start, *The Rise, The Fall, and The Rise*

'The Fall operate like an old-fashioned factory: Smith is the site manager, responsible for hiring and firing workers and overseeing their performances.'

Dave Simpson, *The Fallen*

'Mark E. has always run his band in much the same way that Margaret Thatcher runs her Cabinet, ditching anyone with too strong a mind of their own.'

Dave Jennings, *Melody Maker*, September 1990

'It's become almost a kind of joke, except of course to the people concerned. By and large, people disappear without a trace ... I don't know whether he's killing them, or what.'

John Peel speaking in *The Wonderful and Frightening World of Mark E. Smith*, BBC4 Documentary, 2005

'She has kept the whole thing from collapsing many times. Also known as Kray Carroll and "O.K." Embassy Extra Mild smoker and a former nurse, which probably helps a lot.'

On Kay Carroll in *Bingo-Master's Breakout* press release, June 1978

'Ex rock'n'roll revival group. He got tired of playing "It's Now or Never" every night with inadequate musicians scared of their own hands.'

On Mike Leigh in *Dragnet* press release, November 1979

Is The Shipping Clerk Out There?

Did you hear them Roxy, C A P T CAN on music a week later.
Reading about the scam drop shipments, A N AM zone debaser.
Prices rising when nothing is there to actually purchase…

Yeah scamming those wanting, some fool may pay, then they order.
As it stands would the shipping clerk have allowed this to pass?
Those scum drop shipments not so pleasant in these days passing.

Let's get to work remembering the last gig of the century.
Searing highlight in a memory of blasts,
a loud hailer and the tape recorder, just beating the drum.

Hip Priest has now gone and done a side skip,
spirit slipping through the pub doors and walls.
On the record the repetition keeps grinding.

Were all F A L L /ing \ just keeping,
authentic outings in circumstantial heights.
Taking the bus out passed the by passed.

Seeing I've been sent a message yeah,
having 24 hours to confirm the account, excuse me there.
Hey there scam in yr spam, that's not likely now is it?

That H I P Priest soul split seeing through the day.
I've got this attitude in me, a not having it kind of way.
Now I'm standing up to that fleecing coming on.

On repeat it's taking over,
hey there in bursts\,
HEY \ THEREs …are Spreading…
Its ever so much building a knowledge, appreciating.

Is that Shipping Clerk Out There?

George E. Harris

Late Fall, Early Winter
Blurring, Blindness and Blizzards in *Fall Heads Roll*

Tom Clayton

THE EARLY 2000s were an especially fruitful time for Fall fans – but 2005 really was something else. In January that year, Castle Music re-issued 1982's high-watermark *Hex Enduction Hour*, an album that even Mark E. Smith begrudgingly ranks among his band's best, to rapturous critical re-acclaim. Then, in April, Castle also put out *The Complete Peel Sessions*, a comprehensive chronicle of their appearances on John Peel's Radio 1 show, in the wake of Peel's untimely death the previous October. As if all that wasn't enough, Slogan, under license from Narnack Records in the US, released *Fall Heads Roll* in the UK, a record of new material that found Smith at his coruscating, mischievous and belligerent best – and with a refreshed lineup capable of conjuring a backdrop that was by turns melancholic and pulverising. As a 17-year-old aspirational cynic only just discovering that there were *further alternatives* to 'alternative' music, I was equally beguiled and baffled by this sequence of Fall releases. They were all so very good; why were my peers oblivious to them? Why, more to the point, weren't they the biggest band in the world?

In subsequent months and years, as I discovered more about the band's chequered history and vast discography, I began to see how lucky I had been to first encounter The Fall at this point – with affection for their back catalogue growing in the wake of the Sanctuary reissues, *Fall Heads Roll* arguably representing the zenith of their modern-day revival, and a number of important contemporary bands (including Franz Ferdinand, against whom Smith later threatened legal action for 'mentioning our name') citing the band as a key influence. In fact, that record bucked an unfortunate pattern of Smith often wilfully dismantling the public goodwill or critical momentum that built up during the band's successful periods – usually by putting out a particularly gruelling album, or by amplifying his unfortunate tendency towards erratic and aggressive behaviour on tour or in interviews. While this was far from a hard-and-fast rule (there are none of those when it comes The Fall's output), it wouldn't have been surprising if *Fall Heads Roll* – which followed 2003's delightful and surprising *Real New Fall LP* – had been a difficult listen in the vein of *Room to Live* (1982's hurried and slapdash follow-up to *Hex Enduction Hour*) or *Are You Are Missing Winner* (the near-impenetrable successor to 2001's *The Unutterable*). It turned out to be quite the opposite.

The album's title is indicative of the new, strange position of favour that The Fall and Smith found themselves in at this point. 'Fall Heads Roll' is that rarest of things: a self-referential Fall joke, alluding to Smith's well-documented practice of abruptly firing and replacing band members, a tradition that dated back even as early as the band's formative year. Much (perhaps too much) has been made of the process in the past. And while Smith was undoubtedly difficult to work with, it's also undeniable that there was method behind this apparent madness: a kind of psychic pollarding, a severing of branches to allow new growth, both within the band and within himself; room to live, indeed. There's a telling image on the album's artwork: a coat of arms featuring a benev-olent-looking royal, ship's wheel in one hand, sword raised in the other. Was this how Smith ultimately saw himself, guiding the good ship Fall through thunderstorms largely of his own creation, equally steering and skewering his latest cohort? Whatever the truth, it seems clear that Smith was now increasingly aware of his place in the annals of music history – and was relaxed enough at this point to have a little fun with his dogmatic reputation.

However, the band's new-found status as critical darlings also seemed to set off warning bells in Smith's head. Universally lauded for his lyricism and delivery, on *Fall Heads Roll* Smith consolidates a vocal style glimpsed on *The Real New Fall LP* – a sloppy garbling of words that requires the listener to engage in a fair amount of lyrical guesswork. 'Pacifying Joint' is a good example on this record: even though Smith repeats the title as the song closes, you'd be hard pushed to work out the phrase without a cue from the album artwork. Smith had long experimented with the blurring of meaning and syntax; now those experiments were taken one step further: the words themselves were decaying before our ears. It is, of course, highly debatable how intentional this innovation was; an instinctive reaction to his new-found status as a kind of post-punk poet laureate – or simply a physical side-effect of a decades-long liquid diet? In any case, this blurring brings the desired effect: we listen closer; we are made to work hard to find clarity. Maybe, just maybe, this is what being in The Fall feels like.

Smith's obfuscating delivery stands in sharp contrast to the sensationally sharp playing on *Fall Heads Roll*. One song in particular is a standout achievement – and while it does seem perverse to extol the virtues of a bassline in a book celebrating Smith's words, the bassline in 'Blindness' is no ordinary bassline (and surely a little perversion should be encouraged when discussing The Fall anyway). 'Blindness' is a sonic assault from the very first, but its true brilliance becomes apparent after exactly thirty-four seconds: that's when the rest of the band drops away, leaving just the drums and that insistent, teeth-shoogling bass. It undoubtedly owes a debt to Roots Manuva's 'Witness (1 Hope)', but whereas Rodney Smith's line lollops and bounces, Steve Trafford's variation drives forward with relentless precision. It provides a rock-solid base for Smith's blunted tale of a man driven indoors by both a strict curfew and by a haunting vision of a blind man 'encapsulated in plastic' asking him if he 'works hard'. Over the next seven minutes that scene is re-presented multiple times, with Smith adding and removing detail on each occasion, like a director trying out different angles, testing for impact on each occasion. It's a dazzling update on the band's core ethos of repetition. In fact, 'Blindness' is not just a Great Late Fall Song, but one of the greatest Fall songs ever.

There are further references to obscured vision elsewhere on *Fall Heads Roll* – the fog that 'sticks around' on the imagist short story 'Midnight in Aspen' being a particularly vivid example – but it's the irresistibly bleak 'Early Days of Channel Führer', sitting ominously near end of the album, that fully pulls the wool over our eyes. Framed by uncharacteristically fragile guitar lines, and tapped out in hesitant waltz-time, Smith invites us into a frigid otherworld where 'the snow is all around … like my hand / hat [Fall fans claim both] … it is also white'. It is a fractured and isolationist narrative: 'No coffee for me / no room clearance for me … my only pal is / for I am he'. It is most likely an attempt to depict Adolf Hitler's early days as an aspiring artist in Vienna, which, as one poster on *The Annotated Fall* points out, would explain the waltz-time, too. However, the imagery is obscure enough that 'Early Days …' could just as easily be autobiographical – a rare personal dispatch from what must have often been a lonely psychological eyrie. On an album of calculated risks, this is the greatest – yet it works spectacularly.

For all its dark imagery, however, *Fall Heads Roll* is often a riot. The band's cover of The Move's 'I Can Hear the Grass Grow' is perhaps even more enjoyable than the original; 'Ride Away', with its deadpan 'hey, hey's is just about the oddest opening track you'll ever hear on a Fall album; hell, Mark even lets someone else have a go on the mic for the dramatic dentist-based horror 'Trust in Me'.

As Mark and The Fall approached their own titular season, they couldn't have come up with a better soundtrack with which to rage against the dying of the light. The message from *Fall Heads Roll* was clear: winter may be approaching … but not just yet.

104   Salford, 15 August 2006. Left to right: guitarist Ben Pritchard, keyboard player Elena Poulou, bassist Steve Trafford, Mark E. Smith and drummer Spencer Birtwistle. *Kevin Cummins/Getty Images*

'Some bands have riots when people leave. I remember when Karl left the group before in 1980 and we went on stage with Mike Leigh who's this big sort of chubby teddy boy who used to stand up and never play his bass drum. People in the audience wanted to kill him!

One Two Testing, June 1986

'I've often compared The Fall to an office from hell; me, Simon and Craig are the typing pool, Steve's the office manager, Brix was the P.A. and Mark's the boss, who was in his office.'

Marcia Schofield, *BitchMental*, April/May 1990

'The current lineup of the band (last
    Friday, that is) ...'

Beggars Banquet press clipping, UK,
May 1984

'Smith is currently looking for a full-time
guitarist but says he's toying with the idea
of using ten guitarists when The Fall play
live again.'

NME, July 1998

'I sometimes give the group the wrong address for the studio. Because by the time they find it, they're really annoyed. They play better that way.'

Guardian, May 2001

'Mark's only got two films. *Zulu* or *The Producers*... our punishment for doing a "bad" gig. Tons of Hitlers arabesque across the stage like Michael Clark clones with small square 'taches. "Haa ha ha haha," laughs Mark, nudging me jovially. "Why aren't you laughing?"'

Steve Hanley, *The Big Midweek*

'There's still this trio of me, Craig and Steve that's still the basis of it. Drums and that affects the timings and makes it a bit tighter and stuff. For this thing with oboes I got this girl who used to play the oboe at school, and who's now playing with Martin Bramah in an experimental film band. It's better than getting one of those old codgers out of the pub. Last time I did that, getting a saxophonist in for "Bremen Nacht", he nearly died. The riff was too fast for him.'

Sounds, June 1989

110 Mark with Brix Smith, Manchester, 17 October 1987. On the wall behind them is a painting by Danish artist Claus Castenskiold. *Steve Pyke/Getty Images*

EVERYTHING IS A BLUR before I suddenly realise where I am. There's a mass of equipment. To my right, two guitarists. To my left, a bass player who is shrouded by a stack of amps. All around there is music. What am I doing here? I get a feeling I shouldn't be here at all … a feeling forcibly rammed home by a figure walking towards me in a white shirt.

Now I realise where I am.

The Fall's stage.

His stage.

And I shouldn't be here at all.

I feel a shove beneath my ribcage. 'Get off my fucking stage.' Then all becomes blackness.

I wake up to be confronted by another omnipresent figure in my life – it's Guinness, nestled beneath my ribcage. I've fallen asleep and been dreaming about The Fall.

It's happening a lot lately. Sometimes, I remember what life was life before I started on this biblical quest, before almost every waking hour was spent finding The Fallen. But I can't think about that now. I have to get myself together. The Fall are playing 26 miles away at Leeds Irish Centre, which for some reason has become the only venue The Fall ever play in Leeds, and I have to go.

Several hours later, I'm showered, dressed, *Fall Heads Roll*'s on the car stereo and I'm pulling into the Irish Centre car park for my third Fall gig this year, which must be something like the twenty-ninth or thirty-second Fall gig of my life. Soon enough, I'm in the company of around a thousand cult followers. Among the audience are Hells Angels, blokes with strange facial expressions who look like they've been released from somewhere for the day, teenage girls, bald men and, bizarrely, most of the cast of *Emmerdale*. Who would have thought Paddy the vet and Jimmy King the high-rolling, crooked incompetent would spend evenings listening to The Fall? It's exactly how Kay Carroll described Fall gigs in the 1970s and 1980s – as if a plane had crashed and passengers stumbled to the gig.

Dave Simpson *The Fallen*

In 2005, Dave Simpson embarked on a mission to track down every departed member of The Fall, an epic quest resulting in his 2008 book *The Fallen*. In it, he recounts his journey into *The Weird and Frightening World of The Fall* and manages to meet almost every former band member, with just a few exceptions.

To The Fallen

Definitions
Of poet
Of poetry
Should not be
Defined
By literati
But by us
Laid down
By the regular
Otherworldly
As in
Reel to reel in
Salfordian spiel that
Throws itself up
On Bier Keller floor
As it's
Amped up to
12 times 12 times
Repeat
The smart white
Ringmaster
Shirts the issue
Runs rings
Round the carousel
Beat
As it's
Electric tonight
It's town hall

Crap tonight
It's tight
It's shite
It's one man highlight
As we
Love to
Tot up scores
To compare
Legacy
To examine
Cause
As the
Telly screen shouts
The staccato
Oddball
Vidiprinter slurs
Late
Kick off
Late
Late
Kick off

Mark Coverdale

'The thing about the final stooge, Spencer Birtwistle, is he's a Haçienda casualty; and not only that, he's a drummer as well.'

Renegade

The Fall
At The Zodiac, Oxford 1989

Art Lagun *Nightshift*

KNOWING THAT FALL gigs are populated almost exclusively by men in slightly shabby black clothes I donned the brightest day-glo top I could find. Edinburgh's Foil warm us up with a noisy and impressive racket, sounding like they were raised on a diet of Sonic Youth and Big Black, with supplements of Wire. Their best moments involve frenetic instrumental bursts of energy as evidenced on current single 'Reviver Gene' but lack the raw emotive power of the aforementioned influences.

So how do you review a band you've followed for nineteen years and seen over twenty times? I could start with a highly subjective history of The Fall. Emerged from the Manchester punk scene of 1977 but even then staked an early claim as perpetual outsiders. Early recordings were astonishingly innovative, though concept of lo-fi sometimes taken to literal, i.e. barely audible, extremes. Peaked in early 80s with *Hex Induction Hour* LP before making the fatal mistake of starting to write 'proper' songs and singing them in tune. Lost their way in late 80s like most of their punk contemporaries, only to bounce back in the early 90s with masterpieces like *Shift-Work* and *Code: Selfish*. Now in comfortable position of revered elder statesmen, despite continuing regular changes in line-up and record label.

From the opening moments of 'Pearl City' it's clear we're in for something special. The Fall have always sounded best in small clubs where the crystal-clear mix isn't top priority and you can count the lines on Mark E. Smith's increasingly craggy face. Absent is drummer Simon Wolstencroft but original member Karl Burns more than makes up, punishing his kit as only he can. New guitarist Tommy Crooks has a harder job and struggles visibly, though Julia Nagle on keyboards looks increasingly confident. After a superb 'Idiot Joy Showland' we get a couple of songs off the new album before they cheer up the faithful with 'Lie Dream of a Casino Soul'. Smith looks drunk and happy, which is a good sign, considering it's less than two weeks since he sacked the entire band, albeit briefly. Some songs were supposed to be played along to a DAT but no one seems to know when to start or stop and beats crash into each other but it serves only to add to the air of cheerful chaos. Almost unbelievably they play 'Hip Priest', the legendary epic that Jonathan Demme used in the final basement scene of *Silence of the Lambs*. For surprise value alone it was like watching Hurricane #1 do 'Drive Blind'. Newer songs, 'Oleano' and 'M5' hammer home the point that through all the ups and downs the Fall are still completely without peer. As if for old time's sake Smith has a go at drummer Burns: 'A bit faster this time; I know it's winter but fuckin' hell!'

Despite the dodgy mix, false starts and fuck-ups this is possibly the best gig I've seen The Fall play. A timely reminder never to write off a band when there's still breath in them.

'I'm not having people slag off Brix. Her contribution was amazing – she took the band by the neck and fucking organised it.'

Vox, June 1991

THE LIST OF REMAINING FALLEN is growing ever shorter, but I'm still drawing a blank with Karl Burns. It's rather worrying. How can someone apparently so colourful simply disappear? Worrying about Burns doesn't just keep me up some nights but creeps into my days when I least expect it. One afternoon in Bowden, near Altrincham in Cheshire, I'm interviewing Johnny Marr from The Smiths when we get onto The Fall. It turns out the 'greatest guitarist of our generation' – as Marr is often called – is a Fall fan too. We talk about Fall guitarists we have loved – he is a particular fan of Craig Scanlon – and gigs we have seen. Marr reveals he used to know The Fall almost as much as I did. Who would have ever thought the twangy Smiths' early singles or the darker terrain of later albums *The Queen Is Dead* or *Strangeways, Here We Come* could – somewhere in there – bear the DNA of The Fall?

Karl Burns crops up, because Marr is as mystified as I am. It transpires Marr knew Burns quite well, before The Smiths, when Marr worked in the clothes shop run by Smiths manager Joe Moss. Burns was an erratic customer, obviously before the days when he toured America armed only with a pair of underpants.

'I sold him a leather jacket from the shop, probably '81, '82,' Marr says. 'When I bumped into him ten years later he was still wearing that jacket.' I suppose the moral is: find the jacket, find the man.

I go home and decide to have another go at being Fallen Private Eye. Buried deep in an old Directory of Enquiries for Manchester is an address for one 'Karl E Burns'. It's worth a shot.

The address is in a rundown estate in Ancoats, just off the Oldham Road, which stretches from the city centre to Middleton and Failsworth. Because my Punto blew up one of my many journeys to find The Fall, I've just invested in a new car – a green MG – that sparkles as I creep through the streets. Lovely car, but the last thing you want to be driving in an area like this, because it sticks out like a classical guitarist in The Fall.

The streets are strewn with litter. Half the houses are boarded up. I'm travelling at around five miles per hour because I'm struggling to find the street and feel like a kerb-crawler. And I'm attracting attention. Lots of attention. Some of it comes from the disturbingly young but worldly-looking kinds who ride BMX bikes on the pavement – the traditional form of courier used by Manchester's drug gangs. But most comes from the police, who I notice in the rear-view mirror have taken up a similar pace directly behind my car. They follow me at five miles per hour and have just started to gaze even more intently when I decide to cut my losses and head off. If Karl Burns is there, he is safe from me. For now.

Dave Simpson *The Fallen*

MANCHESTER

Barring brief stints in Edinburgh and Los Angeles, Mark spent his whole life in and around Manchester. He had a fractious and uncomfortable relationship with his home city, often criticising it, while at the same time claiming he could never live anywhere else. It's this tension that informs much of The Fall's best work – from the wiry, snotty chorus of 'Industrial Estate' to the widescreen, quasi-anthemic 'Hit The North'. Angered and baffled by both the rise of the 'baggy' movement in the late eighties, and the rise of the gastropub in the noughties, Mark nevertheless retained a glowering, reluctant pride in Manchester until the very end …

'Every building I ever have from Prestwich on the back of my covers gets fucking pulled down. The church on *Grotesque* is probably one of the few photographs left of the thing. Like the building on "Elastic Man" was pulled down, the building on *Hex Enduction Hour* was pulled down, the building on *Dragnet* was pulled down, [laughs] it's unbelievable. All these places I cherish are pulled down. I chose them because they are good.'

BravEar, Winter 1986

'They're pretty used to [being skint] up here. You can still get pissed for four quid. You can't in London. I always feel a bit sorry for Londoners. You must have to keep earning money just to keep up.'

NME, June 1985

'My basic attitude is that I'd rather live here than in the South and it always has been. I don't really care where anybody lives, though, and I think this North/ South divide is nonsense. I don't envy anyone who lives in Reading, Swindon, or Northampton; they're horrible new towns and the people there are spiritually dead.'

Debris, November 1987

'Most of [the people of Manchester] don't appreciate what's on their own doorstep or they don't until it appears in the evening news and all that shit. It's real then. And they don't appreciate the fact that we've stuck around here, living here.'

City Life, July 1986

'I went to the Haçienda the other day... it's so commercialised – guys who should be ashamed of themselves, well over our ages, with beer bellies and that, blokes I've known for years in, like, electric-green shirts!'

Q, October 1990

'I don't know what the fuck it was. I've been wearing baggy trousers since I was about fucking 16 ...'

Mark when asked about the 'baggy' movement, *Select*, January 1992

'Mark E. Smith – can he even play the fucking guitar? That's what I was brought up on: interesting people in the music business who weren't aimed at the mainstream.'

Noel Gallagher in
The Quietus, February 2015

'I'm very glad now that I stated at the beginning of the year that The Fall want no part of the Manchester scene. You wouldn't believe it up here. I go out to a club, and people look at what shirt I've got on and write it down so the Happy Mondays and The Charlatans can wear one.'

Sounds, December 1990

'I watched a TV programme recently on rock family trees in Manchester. It was all Happy Mondays, Stone Roses and the like. The Fall wasn't featured at all. I thought that was a major achievement.'

Dazed & Confused, November 1998

'Manchester pubs are full of people pretending to be in Oasis, wearing raincoats in July and shouting.'

Select, September 1996

'Manchester's a shit-hole, man. That's what all my songs are about, about how crap the place is. I'm trying to warn people, if you think about it.'

Big Issue, August 1996

'On the 1980 record, *Totale's Turns*, the song "New Puritan" – recorded au naturel in Smith's home – is interrupted when our hero is attacked by a drunk, which, as the sleeve notes immortally explain, "accounts for the tension on that track".'

Bruce Dessau, *The Listener*, March 1988

'I'm completely honest with him all the time, and I don't always take his side. The Mark I read about isn't the Mark I know, because I always know what stage he's going through. They do write an awful lot of rubbish though.'

Mike Pitris, *Select*, 1994

'What my dad would have said was, "God help us if we have a war." Which is what I have started saying. But I always take his advice about these things. He'd always say, "If you're feeling too sexy have a glass of water and a run round the backyard."'

Independent, December 2002

'It's a bit corny, but they've got the language down pat. You hear a slang word in a pub or shop in Manchester, you'll hear it in *Coronation Street* three weeks later. They're really on the ball, quite frightening sometimes.'

Mark on *Coronation Street*, *NME*, September 1992

'Q. Who would you most like to assassinate?

A. Nobody, really, to be quite honest. I don't believe in assassination. I was very tempted to shoot the Pope in 1982 but I grew out of it.'

Smash Hits 'Personal File', May 1987

Twice

Karren Ablaze!

I WAS A CHILD.

It was a rainy night.

No one knew where I was.

I was, of course, at Manchester's Royal National College of Music, watching avant-garde ballet dancer Michael Clark cavort to the music of The Fall.

Was he wearing his trademark assless pants? I think so, but it was not the night's main headfuck.

That was something that happened in the corridor just before the show. It consisted of the approach of two startling individuals, Mr and Mrs Mark E. Smith and Brix! Caught in the headlights of this unmissable pair, I did the only thing a bunny rabbit could do. I proffered myself on their demonic altar. I said hello.

Four eyes feasted upon me. 'CHARMED to meet ya,' they gleamed. And two hands shot forward in fran-tic business-like gestures.

I had to shake them.

As though I was a person worth greeting with such formality. As though I were a grown up.

Their fierce jollity resembled that of a manic fairground horseride. The glazed patterns of multicoloured seaside rock swirled in their irises. Mr Pharmacist had clearly delivered. But at that tender stage I could only surmise what might be the main intention of those proffered paws: intimidation.

The worst of it was that I had been holding a wet umbrella in my hand-shaking hand and Mr Smith in his haste had not given me adequate time to dry it fully on my school gaberdine. Thus my meeting with the hallowed man was marred, for me, by my shame at the inescapably clammy wetness of the palm he grasped.

And then they were gone.

Perhaps, next time I see him, I'll do better.

2.

I was a grown up.

It was a balmy night.

Who cared where I was?

I was, of course, at Leeds's Duchess of York, where The Fall were about to play. Soon that womblike venue would be scooped out and thrown into a skip, and the revealed space within turned into a shit clothes shop – Hugo Boss, AKA Nazi Outfitters. But at that moment it was holding its space between an old man pub and a kebab shop. Things were still real.

I didn't have to do it, this time. I didn't need to put myself in Mark's way. He wasn't milling around, looking for anyone to intimidate. He was tucked away, minding his own business, as was his right.

The stage door was, in my memory, perpetually unguarded. I stepped through into an external yard, and bounded up the stairs behind the bar. Straight ahead, the dressing room door, open. Straight inside, Mark E. Smith, standing in the room.

Now I am fully grown, the ed. of a mag of my own. Perhaps we can finally have a conversation.

'Hello! Mark! I hope you don't mind me intruding. I met you about eighteen years ago, at the Michael Clark performance in Manchester.'

Mark E. Smith raises his eyebrows.

He takes a few steps across the muggy old carpet. Not so steadily; it seems he's all about the booze nowadays.

He leans over to peer down the back of the fridge, as though there is something rather fascinating to be found in the spiderwebby grime between it and the wall.

And offers me his favourite syllable:

'Uh.'

Visitor

Fair Isle, Fair Isle, Fair Isle.
Feral, Feral.
Vistor. Visitor. Visitor.
Space reserved for, Visitor.
Land, reserved for, Visitor.
Visitor to what?
Special Revelation.
The planet, the country, the organisation.
Reserved for what?
Visitors only welcome.
The eternal visitor, will always arrive, and always,
leave.

Dan Cohen

'I was waiting for Andy Votel outside a bar called Night & Day in Manchester and he staggered out of the bar, opened my car door, got in and said, "Take me to Stockport" – so I did, for a laugh.'

Damon Gough, Q, December 2002

'I fancy being a bus conductor ... bit of peace.'

Mark on his post-Fall plans, *Lime Lizard*, May 1993

'I like summer very much, because I never go out in summer. Once April starts, people go out like dogs, so I stay in. Summer is hell.'

NME, May 1999

Mark E Smith

On January 24 Mark E Smith of The Fall died aged 60. He was a long-term reader of WSC and made some contributions to the magazine. In WSC 35 (January 1990) he sent in some of his embarrassing moments for our regular column of that name, reprinted below.

And here are some more, courtesy of Mark E Smith, who admits to:

1. Leading the chant of "*We held 'em to a draw*" at the school canteen after Man City had drawn 0-0 at home to Fenerbahce of Turkey in the European Cup.

2. Writing 'Catholic Gits' on the back of a Man Utd Italian Supporters' coach at a service station on the M6.

3. Going for a job at Louis Edwards' meat factory HQ, getting it, then trying to get out of it, even if they did offer me £8.50 per week plus a season ticket to Man Utd.

4. Seeing George Jones of Bury *jogging* in a local park.

5. Lying to schoolmates that my Dad was a director of Bury and getting found out.

6. Shouting "*Pieface!*" at Prestwich Heys' centre forward during a game v Sutton Utd and getting punched. Then, at the same match, invading the pitch and getting arrested by the navvy who lived at the top of our street who also happened to be a weekend copper...

I CONTACTED MARK SMITH after seeing an interview in *Melody Maker* 1989 where he quoted something that had been written in *WSC* (I've attached that). So we started sending him the magazine each month.

We received regular Christmas cards and the occasional letter and CD over the next twenty years or so. He also sent me a football shirt once, of Hearts, when he was living in Edinburgh briefly after one of his marriages ended. I only met him twice, one to do an interview for *WSC* in 2000, and the other when he turned up unexpectedly for one of our book launches.

He had a reputation for being fierce, but all our contacts with him were these friendly and conversational messages. I didn't tell many people about them at the time because it was just a personal thing he did, not as 'Mark Smith, rock star'.

Andy Lyons, editor of *When Saturday Comes*

FOOTBALL

Mark's lifelong enthusiasm for football, and especially for Manchester City and England, can be traced to his childhood, when he would watch City from the famed Kippax end at Maine Road – experiences which informed The Fall's 1983 single 'Kicker Conspiracy'. A regular reader of the 'half-decent football magazine' *When Saturday Comes*, and an avid viewer of *Match of the Day*, Mark especially loved to hate our national team as much as the next person – but his crowning glory would come when he was asked to read out the classified results on *Final Score* in 2005. It went about as well as could be expected...

'There's two things that people … or, that young men can do to get out of the class system. One is getting into football, and one is to join a group.'

Interview with J. Neo Marvin, jneomarvin.com, 1981

'In football, [The Fall]'d be the "sleeping giants", Wednesday or Derby County …'

David McCullough, *Sounds* gig review, April 1983

'I had a fucking game of football last week and that killed me. It was terrible, the legs were killing me! I still haven't recovered.'

Sounds, July 1986

'The England team are all bloody minor executives who can't kick the ball in the back of the net, can't do the bloody job they're hired to.'

NME, February 1989

'They can't even put away chances from a couple of yards, this England team. I could finish off some of them, and I stopped playing football when I was 14, after I broke a guy's leg.'

Melody Maker, November 1988

'This is why we came fourth. These bastards should have been doing some training, not singing on a bleeding pop record.'

Mark on 'World in Motion', *NME*, December 1990

'Tony Coleman: the Manchester City left winger from 1967-70. He was the wild man of City – the Keith Moon of soccer – completely ungovernable … I used to remember him when I used to watch City in those days and they were like a team full of freaks.'

Melody Maker,
September 1986

'Like I say, United isn't exactly my favourite team, but George Best was in a class of his own. They hounded him out of football because he was far too talented. In him there's the story of British soccer – anyone with any talent was mercilessly gunned down ...'

Melody Maker,
September 1986

'Let's face it, you don't think your ordinary feller with two or three kids, who is actually a soccer fan, can afford to go over to Italy? They're all stockbrokers, journalists and fucking cunts.'

Melody Maker, December 1997

'You can bet some strange things go on behind the doors of the FA. They're like a cult; a randy cult souped-up on good wine, expensive fruit and nice clean sausages.'

Renegade

'The local paper had a "where are they now?" feature recently on City's team from the Rodney Marsh time in the early 1970s. There were a couple who just seem to have disappeared off the face of the earth. One was quoted as saying "if I wasn't a footballer I'd be a tramp" and I think he's done it.'

When Saturday Comes, March 2000

'My mates have been out for a drink with Malcolm Allison, talking about Man City. At the end of the night he takes his hat off and expects you to put 20 quid in – for the pleasure of his company. It's like me having a chat here now and asking for 50 quid at the end. Maybe I should start doing that.'

Word, January 2006

'The annoying thing about that Beckham foul in the World Cup, when he got sent off, was he hardly even kicked him. If you're going to kick them, kick them.'

When Saturday Comes, March 2000

'I do know quite a few Greek football fans ... and their attitude to soccer is completely different to Britain's. It's not about winning. It's just about being within the club. They find British fans very funny. They find them hilarious – you know, when they cry.'

Independent, June 2004

CLASSIFIED FOOTBALL RESULTS, Saturday 19th November 2005, as read by Mark E. Smith

Premiership

Charlton Athletic 1 – 3 Manchester United
Chelsea 3 – 0 Newcastle United
Liverpool 3 – 0 Portsmouth
Manchester City* 0 – 0 Blackburn Rovers
(*'hopeless as usual')
Sunderland 1 – 3 Aston Villa
Tottenham P – P West Ham*
(*Mark reads '1h' as West Ham's score,
referring to their Pools code)
West Bromwich Albion 0 – 0 Everton
Wigan Athletic 2 – 3 Arsenal

Championship

Burnley 1 – 0 Leicester City
Coventry City 1 – 1 Ipswich Town
Crewe Alexandra 1 – 2 Stoke City
Norwich City 2 – 0 Luton Town
Plymouth Argyle 3 – 1 QPR
Preston North End 2 – 1 Cardiff City
Reading 3 – 1 Hull City
Sheffield United 2 – 2 Millwall
Southampton ('…town') 3 – 4 Leeds United
Watford 2 – 1 Sheffield Wednesday

League One

Barnsley 1 – 1 Rotherham United
Brentford 3 – 3 Oldham Athletic
Bristol City 2 – 4 Chesterfield ('…town')
Colchester United 3 – 2 Blackpool
Doncaster Rovers 4 – 2 Bournemouth
Gillingham 1 – 0 Hartlepool United
Huddersfield Town 0 – 0 Bradford City
Milton Keynes Dons 2 – 1 Walsall
Nottingham Forest 2 – 0 Southend United
Port Vale 1 – 1 Swindon Town
Scunthorpe United 1 – 2 Tranmere Rovers

League Two

Barnet 1 – 0 Torquay United
Boston United 1 – 2 Notts County
Bury P – P Rushden & Diamonds
Carlisle United 2 – 1 Oxford United
Leyton Orient 2 – 2 Stockport County
Macclesfield Town 1 – 0 Darlington
Northampton Town 4 – 0 Bristol Rovers*
(*Mark omits 'Rovers' here)
Rochdale 2 – 2 Chester City
Shrewsbury Town P – P Mansfield Town
Wrexham 1 – 1 Peterborough United
Wycombe Wanderers 3 – 1 Grimsby Town

In the subsequent interview, Mark asks Ray Stubbs why he has a 'number one haircut' … 'you look like a murderer from Strangeways'.

Mark and Steve Hanley on bass performing at the ICA, London, UK, 18 June 1980.
David Corio/Redferns/Getty Images

MISCELLANEOUS JUKEBOX

Mark's responses to interview questions were often as uncategorisable as his band's output; no aspect of life escaped his all-seeing, all-critical eye. The following is a selection of his more leftfield fixations, including *Big Brother* and *The Weakest Link*, as well as roast beef sandwiches, milk adverts and *Titanic*.

'I always feel deeply sorry for people from Northampton … I remember when I was about 20, I'd been a vegetarian for two years and this gig we did in Northampton was so chaotic I just went into a Wimpy bar and ate five burgers!'

Select, 1990

'It's very bad for you being a veggo. It makes your brain go funny because it's not getting any protein.'

The Hit, October 1985

'If Jesus had seen U2 he'd have been very mad indeed. Jesus would throw bottles at U2.'

Alternative Press, September 1993

'Now Wham[!], I think they're really good. Whatever you say about them that guy's a really good singer. His voice is great and he's dead handsome and all that. Like when he goes on TV everyone screams, I think that's great.'

The Hit, October 1985

'That fucking milk advert with fucking Bob Geldof in it. I mean, what's the point of advertising milk? We've all got to drink it, unless you're some sort of diet freak. It's like advertising music! "Music! Listen to it. Music is good for you!"'

Melody Maker, November 1988

'My roast beef sandwiches have made both grown-up intellectuals and juvenile hoodlums weep with pleasure.'

City Life, August 1999

'[The Libertines] are always going about themselves, aren't they? The music doesn't hold up, I don't think. I think McFly are quite good, though.'

Ice, March 2005

'Sometimes for weeks on end I just watch telly, and after a bit you go "What the fuck am I doing here?" Everybody does it.'

NME, April 1991

'There's one or two that I switch off automatically. That one that's really offensive ... *Kilroy*, that's it. Really offensive. Have you seen that? "If you've ever been a child molester, ring *Kilroy*" ... Bloody hell.'

Melody Maker, April 1991

'I like the way they tackled all the big issues, Boney M. The fall of the Russian tsarist system, and stuff like that.'

Melody Maker, July 1994

'My cat is one of my best friends: he's outlasted any group member or wife. He's about 20 and he looks better than anyone I've played with since 1978. He's got a new lease of life and started jumping up and killing bees.'

NME, December 1998

'I used to get shit in the press for the Armani jumper I used to wear years ago. It was "If he's so scruffy why's he got an Armani jumper?" I bought it in a shop. I saw and liked it ... I just thought it was a marvellous jumper and I've still got it.'

NME, February 1992

'Young people don't know how to walk these days. They spend all their student grants on trendy vitamins and they're all going fucking blind. The bleedin' government needs to take a look at the situation.'

Mark shortly after colliding with a lamppost he mistook for an errant youth, *Frieze*, September 1992

'[John] Major – he's the Antichrist. There's something in Nostradamus about him – "a pearled isle will be destroyed by a man from the circus who has turned to politics."'

NME, May 1994

'People who read *Loaded* are just frustrated perverts like yourself! … you're a fucking dead-leg cunt and I'm not talking to you.'

Loaded, December 1997

'Mark E. Smith could grump for England, but he has his lighter moments. Take the time two weeks ago, when he was visiting the Notting Hill office of his publicist. He was in customarily dour spirits until he spoffed a crane parked next to the building, its operator at the top repairing its scaffolding. He entered the empty cab and spent the next few minutes gleefully raising and lowering the hapless operator. Mark E. Smith is 39.'

Caroline Sullivan, *Guardian*, September 1997

'*Titanic*? What a load of crap. It's like watching a PlayStation. The fucking boat turns over. I mean, you know how it ends, don't you?'

NME, September 1998

'Now it's all retro, innit? And that's why stuff like *Mojo* exists … I throw it in the bin. Use it for cat litter.'

NME, February 1996

'It's like a sort of state-of-the-nation programme, isn't it? People want to be told off nowadays. It's like a reaction against the liberalism of the 1970s and 1980s.'

Mark on the subject of the TV quiz show *The Weakest Link*, Q, May 2001

'Makes me laugh when at the end of *Big Brother* they say you can carry on watching it on your computer. Like somebody might go for a slash and you might miss it. Hahaha!'

Uncut, October 2003

'Nirvana tried to get into our bus, Courtney whatshername, the actress, tried it and we pushed her off. Heh, heh. But they all come from this horrible place called Seattle which is just like Moss Side on a bad night.'

NME, February 1994

'People were coming up to me saying "listen to this", and playing me Pavement records on a Walkman, and I just asked, "What live tape is that of ours? Is that from Holland in 1987 or something?"'

Melody Maker, December 1993

Snakes in my Boots

I've got snakes in my boots
The roots return
The white fire burns
The whistle toots

I've got snakes in my boots
The war on truth
Rages electronic
Pages of History
Flicker and flap
In the wind
The illuminated book
Pimps the mystery
As the Asian girls
Dance in the Celtic nook

I've got snakes in my boots
The quest for home
The search for room
To live and breathe
The sack of Rome
A barbarian frenzy
The slaughter of priests
The laughter it meets
The pristine dawn it greets
A crucial pagan cleansing

I've got snakes in my boots
The roots return
The white fire burns
The whistle toots

Nature is screaming
Nature is howling
Like a jilted banshee
Growling like a hunted wolf
The war on truth
The viral empires
Hypnotise the narcissi
Paralyse desire
Castrate the majesty
Of a golden oak
In a glade at dusk
The tree of life
Chopped into
Discarded IKEA sawdust
Collecting human vomit
In the bar of barren souls

I've got snakes in my boots
The roots return
The white fire burns
The whistle toots

Whistle me a song Maeve
A song of freedom
Something to belong to
Something to hold in a heart
Shattered with hate
As it seeks a home
Or a dreaming grave
I've got snakes in my boots
The roots adore
The white fire roars
The whistle toots

Snow on the rowan tree
Snow on the blackthorn
Cool my face
Clear my head
Chill my glass
Awake the dead

I've got snakes in my boots
A song in my head
To kill the dread
Ten thousand Angels
Dancing on a bin
Ten thousand Angels
Dancing on a bin
Ten thousand Angels
Dancing on a bin ...

Roddy McDevitt

'Young bands come into the studio when you're mixing and they'll ask – they're blatant about it – Oh, what BPM's that in? I go, What the fuck's it got to do with you! Get out!'

Q, May 1992

'I don't stop and think about bettering the last record. It's pointless, isn't it? I've seen too many groups on that track talking about remixes and all that bloody stuff; it's not what The Fall want.'

Indiecator, 1993

'Apparently, all authors write their best novels between 30 and 35. If you father a child at 34 it's gonna be a genius! I know I look a damn sight better now than I did at 22 ... I account it to my high meat diet and high alcohol consumption. Keeps you young. Liquids. Very important.'

NME, January 1990

'[David Bowie] said I write sixth form poetry. I couldn't believe it. And there he is now trying to do "Kurious Oranj" with a white shirt and black trousers. He's a fucking old bastard and I hope you print that.'

NME, July 1989

Mark performing live on stage at the Paradiso in Amsterdam, Netherlands on 23 February 1987.
Frans Schellekens/Redferns

'There was a time when I asked Mark if he'd heard that "Under Pressure" song that Bowie did with Queen and he just said, "Yeah! They ripped that bass-line off 'An Older Lover'."'

Brix Smith Start, *ZigZag*, November 1983

'Fall beseige hit parade with Kinks cover, included here. Purists affronted but Fall pay off Currys fridge and sofa with royalties.'

Mark on *The Frenz Experiment*, *Volume*, September 1992

'I get letters from kids in Wales. Their lives have been transformed by The Fall. I suppose, if you're on the dole in Wales, there's nowt else to do unless you're out burgling.'

Frieze, September 1992

I thought I was going deaf from being on stage. I was shouting at everyone. I was also very unhappy with the sound of the band. I knew something was wrong, but I couldn't hear what it was. The nurse freaked over my ears. She had to pump them out two or three times. She said she'd never seen so much wax. Apparently, I had enough for three 70-year-old blokes.'

Dazed & Confused, November 1998

'I don't think heroin is any good, it's crap, a horrible drug ... Have you ever seen anyone on it? They sweat and snuffle like little piglets. Imagine paying money to be like that, you'll find out what it's like when you're 90 anyway.'

NME, August 1986

'What do you mean by "love"? Love to me is love of life. You see love every day: a dad with his kid, a mother with her kid. It's a question of how you put that down on paper.'

City Life, July 1986

Legend of The Fall

Dave Simpson

first published in the *Guardian*, January 2018

I FIRST MET MARK E. SMITH in 1981, as I waited on the steps of Leeds University, about to see my first ever Fall gig. Suddenly I spied the singer coming out of the building and rushed over to get an autograph. I was a painfully naive schoolboy and had no idea how to approach a pop star – or, rather, an enigmatic cult figure with a fearsome reputation for taking no prisoners. Smith wasn't exactly the darling of the music press but he was viewed with a mixture of curiosity, awe and fear: I'd already read enough about him to know that he was someone whom one should approach as one might a savage dog.

In the event – and this was my first lesson in his unknowability and unpredictability – he could not have been nicer. He didn't have a pen, nor did I, but the previous month I'd met Captain Sensible from the Damned on the steps of Unity Hall in Wakefield, and he'd taken a bite out of my concert ticket in lieu of an autograph. I asked Mark E. Smith to do the same and I still have the perfect paper impression of his 1981 dental work, which presumably contains enough DNA traces for a clone. Not that there could ever be another Mark E. Smith.

I can picture that gig as if it were yesterday. The wilfully unfashionably outfitted Smith was visibly in charge, like a demented building-site foreman, barking out lyrics like they were orders as his band cowered behind him, hammering out a pulverising, hypnotic racket.

Two bands changed my life. Joy Division introduced me to the power of music and the possibilities of sound, and demonstrated that pop songs could be far more – and come from somewhere far deeper and darker – than entertainment. But the Fall changed everything I felt about words and language. From the moment I heard 'Totally Wired' in a friend's cellar

174

at an impressionable age, Smith's lyrics had a seismic effect on me. To listen to my first Fall album, *Grotesque (After the Gramme)* was to enter an unknowable netherworld of 'hydrochloric shaved weirds', 'new faces in hell', hideous replicas of much-loathed dog breeders and a worldview that sneered at Englishmen, councils, rapists, northerners, southerners, students, tourists, dogs and, well, pretty much everyone and everything. This was not the language I knew from pop. It was more like musical science fiction.

I developed an obsession with The Fall that evening in Leeds that has lasted a lifetime. On a good night, with Smith at full pelt and Steve Hanley grappling with the bass like it was a wild animal, they were the best band in the world. On a bad one, they could be an irritable, irascible row. I first vowed to never go and see The Fall again as long ago as 1985, and yet like a dog returning to its vomit, I'd always be drawn back.

They were never quite my favourite band, but were always there or thereabouts, a microcosm of their relationship with the rest of pop. The Fall have had scores of charting records. Meanwhile, key incidents in my own life have been bound up in The Fall: first pint of bitter at that first Fall gig; losing my virginity to the girl who gave me my first Fall album. Later, I went out with a girl called Victoria whose name gave our coupling extra frisson because, well, The Fall were in the charts with a Kinks cover called 'Victoria'.

I've seen Smith deliver a professional performance worthy of Sinatra and gigs that were an epic shambles, with the seemingly drunken singer dismantling the band's gear on stage or 'singing' (or rather, making noises) from the comfort of the dressing room. This, as he well knew, was part of the fascination: you never knew which Smith you would get.

We had two further encounters after that fleeting initial meeting. In 1997, when I nervously conducted a 'pop summit' for *Melody Maker* with Smith, the Beautiful South's Paul Heaton and New Order's Peter Hook, the three luminaries ended up trudging around Manchester because it turned out that Smith had been barred from almost all the city-centre pubs. It ended up in a drinking session that went on for hours, and through the haze I vividly remember Smith devouring poor Heaton. His crime? He confessed to liking the Fall.

After the third and last encounter, in September 2005, our worlds collided in a new way. Because Smith had been interviewed countless times in the *Guardian*, my editor had a new angle: how about getting the singer to talk about the numerous band members he'd fired (or who had fired him) over the years, and then get a few of them to talk about Smith? That plan went awry when Smith refused to divulge the whereabouts of any ex-members. Instead, I tracked them down myself – scouring the internet, old phone books and remote Lancashire hillsides, ending up finding more than 40.

This epic quest destroyed my 17-year relationship, and my girlfriend even dumped me for a lorry driver ('Container Drivers' being my favourite Fall song), but by the time the *Guardian* article became a book, *The Fallen: Life In and Out of Britain's Most Insane Group*, I'd uncovered the jealously guarded inner workings of The Fall, which were as weird as the songs.

Smith ran the group like a small industrial factory, hiring and firing on a whim. I heard from wives and ex-girlfriends, who'd all been ultimately discarded or abandoned by him (one, girlfriend/manager/kazoo soloist Kay Carroll, exited the van on a freeway in the middle of a snowstorm). I heard tales of guitarists being blindfolded on the way to gigs or dumped in Swedish forests; there were stories of 'creative tension' and psychological torture. Songs had been recorded live in the back of speeding vans. A drummer who hadn't played for years found himself press-ganged into The Fall minutes before they played to thousands at Reading, by a singer and guitarist bloodied from going at each other with knuckledusters.

However, Smith was far too complex or intelligent to be a mere ogre. He could be as hilarious as some of the songs (I love the story that the Fall's contract to appear on *Later … with Jools Holland* included a clause stipulating that under no circumstances was Holland to play 'boogie-woogie piano anywhere near The Fall'). Many ex-members had tales of extraordinary generosity and kindness: how he'd come to their aid when they needed it, or taken them around the world. Carroll travelled from the US to visit 'the Smith' (as she calls him) and wounds were healed. Almost all said that The Fall experience had been character-building and most that they'd do it again in a shot.

Granted, this probably didn't apply to one particularly incredulous guitarist, who revealed how an entire Fall lineup abandoned Smith and his latest wife after he poured beer over the head of their coach driver, who was doing 80mph at the time. While some former members needed acupuncture to recover from being in the mighty Fall, Smith merely dusted himself down. The great tracks kept coming (if not, admittedly, as frequently as they once did) and the singer would emerge fronting another set of musicians he'd stumbled upon in the pub.

Of course, it's hard not to think of Smith without thinking of alcohol. He was a hardened drinker (and the rest) from his teens. Interviewing him meant matching him pint for pint (I managed to avoid the whisky chasers) and I can still picture him at that last encounter, cackling as he told me how he used to fine drummer Karl Burns £5 every time he hit the tom tom. After four hours, tape machine off, Smith suggested 'going over the road for one' and I ended up so plastered that it was several hours before I felt able to get back in the car. I'll always remember his last words to me, as he departed in a taxi, as cheery (and, weirdly, seemingly as sober) as he was in 1981: 'Thanks, Dave, I've really enjoyed it.' Then, when the book came out, he annihilated it, announcing: 'I've just fucking burned it.'

He was ever the contrarian, but if there was one thing that was predictable about him, it was his commitment to The Fall. As long ago as 1979, he said that his aim in life was 'to keep it going as long as I can'. It says everything about him that he kept performing until the very bitter end – even visibly ill in a wheelchair. Music has lost one of its most distinctive, inimitable characters.

Attitude

This is the last Fall gig
the bitter fig the twisted cig the rig unrigged
in the stone clink
with the first Fall fan ankle tattoo like biro twigs

No rock no punk no polish no spin no spit

boy in a white shirt
boy in a wooly jumper
rider in two carrier bags
unlikely provider of the last Fall gig
built wheelchair ramp and safe den
on the high stage

queue overlaps around the block
round the stone clink
after the thousand thousand thousand shows
this is no show

sends unlikely love to the empty stage
boy in a white shirt
boy in a wooly jumper

everyone will say they were there but you weren't there either

fans overlap around the block
what will we do now?

spun out and suddenly older
spun out and suddenly older

Pauline Sewards

Mark performing at the Lyceum Theatre, London, on 12 December 1982. *David Corio/Redferns/Getty Images* 179

'I have stood in many dark clubs watching Mark E. Smith prowling the stage amidst a swirl of mic leads and gaffer tape, interfering with speaker knobs, prodding discordantly at keyboards, proclaiming his dark lyrics like a man shouting from a prison window. They were the most exciting music gigs I ever saw or will ever see.

Mark went his own way, regardless of fashion or financial rewards. He produced the most original, thought-provoking, spine-tingling music I've ever heard.

When I finally got to interview him, he turned up an hour late and greeted me with, "Hello, Stewart." I loved him. He was quite simply better than all the rest. I thought he'd live forever. He seemed too belligerent to die. But he has and oh the difference to me.'

Frank Skinner on Absolute Radio, 24 January 2018

SELECTED DISCOGRAPHY

- Studio Albums
- Live/Studio Albums
- Live Albums
- EPs
- Mark E. Smith Spoken Word Albums

The record labels and dates listed here refer to the initial UK release.

Studio albums

Live at the Witch Trials (Step Forward, 1979)
Dragnet (Step Forward, 1979)
Grotesque (After the Gramme) (Rough Trade, 1980)
Slates (Rough Trade, 1981)
Hex Enduction Hour (Kamera, 1982)
Room to Live (Kamera, 1982)
Perverted by Language (Rough Trade, 1983)
The Wonderful and Frightening World Of... (Beggars Banquet, 1984)
This Nation's Saving Grace (Beggars Banquet, 1985)
Bend Sinister (Beggars Banquet, 1986)
The Frenz Experiment (Beggars Banquet, 1988)
I Am Kurious Oranj (Beggars Banquet, 1988)
Extricate (Phonogram, 1990)
Shift-Work (Phonogram, 1991)
Code: Selfish (Phonogram, 1992)
The Infotainment Scan (Permanent/Matador, 1993)
Middle Class Revolt (Permanent/Matador, 1994)
Cerebral Caustic (Permanent, 1995)
The Light User Syndrome (Jet, 1996)
Levitate (Artful, 1997)
The Marshall Suite (Artful, 1999)
The Unutterable (Eagle, 2000)
Are You Are Missing Winner (Cog Sinister/Voiceprint, 2001)

The Real New Fall LP (Formerly Country on the Click) (Action, 2003)
Fall Heads Roll (Slogan, 2005)
Reformation! Post-TLC (Slogan, 2007)
Imperial Wax Solvent (Castle, 2008)
Your Future Our Clutter (Domino, 2010)
Ersatz GB (Cherry Red Records, 2011)
Re-Mit (Cherry Red Records, 2013)
Sub-Lingual Tablet (Cherry Red Records, 2015)
New Facts Emerge (Cherry Red Records, 2017)

Live/Studio Albums

Totale's Turns (Rough Trade, 1980)
Seminal Live (Beggars Banquet, 1989)
The Twenty-Seven Points (Permanent, 1995)
2G+2 (Action, 2002)
Interim (Hip Priest/Voiceprint, 2004)

Live Albums

Live in London 1980 (Chaos Tapes, 1982)
A Part of America Therein, 1981 (Cottage, 1982)
Fall in a Hole (Flying Nun, 1983)
BBC Radio 1 Live in Concert (Windsong International, 1993)
The Legendary Chaos Tape (Scout Releases/Rough Trade, 1996)
In the City ... (Artful, 1997)
15 Ways to Leave Your Man, Live (Receiver, 1997)
Live to Air in Melbourne 1982 (Cog Sinister/Voiceprint, 1998)

Live Various Years (Cog Sinister/Voiceprint, 1998)
Nottingham '92 (Cog Sinister/Voiceprint, 1998)
Live 1977 (Cog Sinister/Voiceprint, 2000)
I Am as Pure as Oranj (Burning Airlines, 2000)
Live in Cambridge 1988 (Cog Sinister/Voiceprint, 2000)
Austurbaejarbio (Live in Reykjavik 1983) (Cog Sinister/Voiceprint, 2001)
Live in Zagreb (Cog Sinister/Voiceprint, 2001)
Liverpool 78 (Cog Sinister/Voiceprint, 2001)
Touch Sensitive ... Bootleg Box Set (Castle, 2003)
The Idiot Joy Show (Alchemy/Burning Airlines, 2003)
Live at the Phoenix Festival (Strange Fruit, 2003)
Pearl City (Roskilde 1996) (Get Back, 2004)
Live at Deeply Vale (Ozit, 2005)
Live from the Vaults – Oldham 1978 (Hip Priest/Voiceprint, 2005)
Live from the Vaults – Retford 1978 (Hip Priest/Voiceprint, 2005)
Live from the Vaults – Los Angeles 1979 (Hip Priest/Voiceprint, 2005)
Live from the Vaults – Glasgow 1981 (Hip Priest/Voiceprint, 2005)
Live from the Vaults – Alter Bahnoff, Hof, Germany 1981
(Hip Priest/Voiceprint, 2005)
Live at the Knitting Factory, New York 9 April 2001
(Hip Priest/Voiceprint, 2007)
Live at the Garage, London 20 April 2002 (Hip Priest/Voiceprint, 2007)
Live at the Knitting Factory, LA 14 November 2001
(Hip Priest/Voiceprint, 2007)
Live at the ATP Festival 28 April 2002 (Hip Priest/Voiceprint, 2007)
Last Night at The Palais (Sanctuary, 2009)

Live in San Francisco (Ozit-Morpheus, 2013)
Live Uurop VIII-XII Places in Sun & Winter, Son (Cherry Red, 2014)
Bingo Masters at the Witch Trials (Dandelion/Ozit-Morpheus, 2016
Live in Clitheroe (Ozit-Morpheus, 2017)

EPs

Bingo-Master's Break-Out! (Step Forward, 1978)
Fiery Jack (Step Forward, 1980)
C.R.E.E.P. (Beggars Banquet, 1984)
Call for Escape Route (Beggars Banquet, 1984)
The Dredger (Cog Sinister/Fontana, 1990)
The Fall vs 2003 (Action, 2002)
(We Wish You) A Protein Christmas (Action, 2003)
Rude (All the Time) (Hip Priest/Voiceprint, 2005)
The Remainderer (Cherry Red Records, 2013)
Wise Ol' Man (Cherry Red Records, 2016)

Mark E. Smith Spoken Word Albums

The Post Nearly Man (Artful, 1998)
Pander! Panda! Panzer! (Action, 2002)

'Does death worry you?'

'Nah … when it comes,
peace will be very
welcome.'

Sounds, August 1983

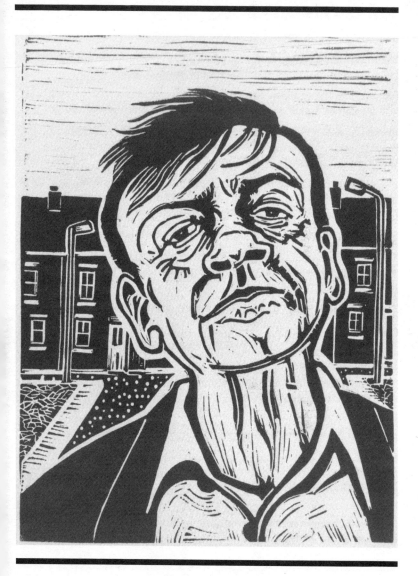

'I'm not fucking signing that.' Mark's initial reaction on being presented with a copy of the linocut. He revised his opinion and said he was 'chuffed' when he realised it was a present from the artist...

Mark E. Smith in Salford, by Ben Dickson

Text Credits

Every effort has been made to contact copyright holders where appropriate, but please contact the publisher if there are any errors or omissions.

Extracts from *Renegade* by Mark E. Smith (Penguin Books, 2009) reproduced with permission from Penguin Books. Copyright © Mark E. Smith, 2008.

Extracts from *The Fallen* by Dave Simpson (Canongate Books, 2008) reproduced with permission from Canongate Books.
Copyright © Dave Simpson, 2008.

Extracts from *The Big Midweek: Life Inside The Fall* by Steve Hanley and Olivia Piekarski (Route Publishing, 2016) reproduced with permission from Route Publishing. Copyright © Steve Hanley and Olivia Piekarski, 2016.

The publisher thanks the following authors for their contributions to the book:

Page 7:
'MES' by Stuart Maconie, copyright © Stuart Maconie, 2018.

Page 13:
'Search: Mark E. Smith' by Paul McGrane, copyright © Paul McGrane, 2018.

Page 16:
'Meeting your Heroes' by Phil Harrison, copyright © Phil Harrison, 2018.

Page 20:
'Summer 2004: MES at the Malmaison' by Tim Cumming,
copyright © Tim Cumming, 2018.

Page 36:
Untitled by Emma Garland, copyright © Emma Garland, 2018.

Page 39:
'Mark flies home to Baby' by Emma Hammond,
copyright © Emma Hammond, 2018. @EHwords

Page 49:
'I kind of expected it but hoped otherwise' by Tim Wells,
copyright © Tim Wells, 2018.